Serbian Vocabulary:
A Serbian Language Guide

Lazar Pavlovic

Contents

List of Serbian letters

Order	Serbian Latin Alphabet	Serbian Cyrillic Alphabet	IPA
1	A a	А а	/ ʌ /
2	B b	Б б	/ b /
3	C v	Ц ц	/ ts /
4	Č č	Ч ч	/ tʃ /
5	Ć ć	Ћ ћ	/ tj /
6	D d	Д д	/ d /
7	Dž dž	Џ џ	/ dʒ /
8	Đ đ	Ђ ђ	/ dj / *
9	E e	Е е	/ e /
10	F f	Ф ф	/ f /
11	G g	Г г	/ g /
12	H h	Х х	/ h /
13	I i	И и	/ ɪ /
14	J j	Ј ј	/ j /
15	K k	К к	/ k /
16	L l	Л л	/ l /
17	Lj lj	Љ љ	/ lj / *
18	M m	М м	/ m /
19	N n	Н н	/ n /
20	Nj nj	Њ њ	/ nj / *
21	O o	О о	/ ɒ /
22	P p	П п	/ p /
23	R r	Р р	/ r /
24	S s	С с	/ s /
25	Š š	Ш ш	/ ʃ /
26	T t	Т т	/ t /
27	U u	У у	/ ʊ /
28	V v	В в	/ v /
29	Z z	З з	/ z /
30	Ž ž	Ж ж	/ ʒ /

* this means that this is one and single sound in Serbian, and these sounds do not have any corresponding counterparts in English. Rather, they can be best expressed through the combination of two sounds which would be uttered/spoken together and quickly as a whole

1) Measurements
Mere
Мере

First Line - Vocabulary Item

Second Line - Serbian Latin

Third Line - Serbian Cyrillic

Fourth Line - Serbian Pronunciation

---

acre

jutro

јутро

/ **jʊ**trɒ /

---

area

područje

подручје

/ **pɒ**drʊtʃje /

---

case

kutija

кутија

/ **kʊ**tɪjʌ /

---

centimeter

centimetar

центиметар

/ **tse**ntɪmetʌr /

---

cup

šolja

шоља

/ ʃɒljʌ /

---

dash

1/8 kašičice = malo

1/8 кашичице = мало

/ 1/8 kʌʃɪtʃɪtse / = / mʌlɒ /

---

degree

stepen

степен

/ **ste**pen /

---

depth

dubina

дубина

/ dʊbɪnʌ /

---

digit

cifra

цифра

/ tsɪfrʌ /

---

dozen

tuce

туце

/ tʊtse /

---

foot

stopa

стопа

/ stɒpʌ /

---

gallon

galon

галон

/ gʌlɒn /

---

gram

gram

грам

/ grʌm /

---

height

visina

висина

/ vɪsɪnʌ /

---

huge

ogromno

огромно

/ ɒgrɒmnɒ /

---

inch

inč

инч

/ ɪntʃ /

---

kilometer

kilometar

километар

/ kɪlɒmetʌr /

---

length

dužina

дужина

/ dʊʒɪnʌ /

---

liter

litar

литар

/ lɪtʌr /

---

little

malo

мало

/ mʌlɒ /

---

measure

mera

мера

/ merʌ /

---

meter

metar

метар

/ metʌr /

---

mile

milja

миља

/ **mil**jʌ /

---

minute

minut

минут

/ **mɪ**nʊt /

---

miniature

minijaturno

минијатурно

/ **mɪ**nɪjʌtʊrnɒ /

---

ounce

unca

унца

/ **ʊ**ntsʌ /

---

perimeter

obim

обим

/ **ɒ**bɪm /

---

pint

pinta

пинта

/ **pɪ**ntʌ /

pound

funta

фунта

/ fʊntʌ /

quart

četvrtina

четвртина

/ tʃetvrtɪnʌ /

ruler

lenjir

лењир

/ lenjɪr /

scale

vaga

вага

/ vʌgʌ /

small

malo

мало

/ mʌlɒ /

tablespoon

kašika

кашика

/ kʌʃɪkʌ /

teaspoon

kašičica

кашичица

/ kʌʃitʃitsʌ /

ton

tona

тона

/ tɒnʌ /

unit

jedinica

јединица

/ jedɪnɪtsʌ /

volume

zapremina

запремина

/ zʌpremɪnʌ /

weigh

težiti

тежити

/ teʒɪtɪ /

weight

težina

тежина

/ teʒɪnʌ /

width

širina

ширина

/ ʃɪrɪnʌ /

---

yard

jard

јард

/ jʌrd /

Time
Vreme
Време

What time is it?

Koliko je sati?

Колико је сати?

/ kɒlɪkɒ je sʌtɪ /

It's 1:00 AM/PM

Sada je 1 prepodne/popodne

Сада је 1 преподне/поподне

/sʌdʌ je 1 **pre**pɒdne/**pɒ**pɒdne /

It's 2:00 AM/PM

Sada je 2 prepodne/popodne

Сада је 2 преподне/поподне

/ sʌdʌ je 2 **pre**pɒdne/**pɒ**pɒdne /

It's 3:00 AM/PM

Sada je 3 prepodne/popodne

Сада је 3 преподне/поподне

/ sʌdʌ je 3 **pre**pɒdne/**pɒ**pɒdne /

It's 4:00 AM/PM

Sada je 4 prepodne/popodne

Сада је 4 преподне/поподне

/ sʌdʌ je 4 **pre**pɒdne/**pɒ**pɒdne /

It's 5:00 AM/PM

Sada je 5 prepodne/popodne

Сада је 5 преподне/поподне

/ sʌdʌ je 5 **pre**pɒdne/**pɒ**pɒdne /

It's 6:00 AM/PM

Sada je 6 prepodne/popodne

Сада је 6 преподне/поподне

/ sʌdʌ je 6 **pre**pɒdne/**pɒ**pɒdne /

It's 7:00 AM/PM

Sada je 7 prepodne/popodne

Сада је 7 преподне/поподне

/ sʌdʌ je 7 **pre**pɒdne/**pɒ**pɒdne /

It's 8:00 AM/PM

Sada je 8 prepodne/popodne

Сада је 8 преподне/поподне

/ sʌdʌ je 8 **pre**pɒdne/**pɒ**pɒdne /

It's 9:00 AM/PM

Sada je 9 prepodne/popodne

Сада је 9 преподне/поподне

/ sʌdʌ je 9 **pre**pɒdne/**pɒ**pɒdne /

It's 10:00 AM/PM

Sada je 10 prepodne/popodne

Сада је 10 преподне/поподне

/ sʌdʌ je 10 **pre**pɒdne/**pɒ**pɒdne /

It's 11:00 AM/PM

Sada je 11 prepodne/popodne

Сада је 11 преподне/поподне

/ sʌdʌ je 11 **pre**pɒdne/**pɒ**pɒdne /

It's 12:00 AM/PM

Sada je 12 prepodne/popodne

Сада је 12 преподне/поподне

/ sʌdʌ je 12 **pre**pɒdne/**pɒ**pɒdne /

---

in the morning

prepodne

преподне

/ **pre**pɒdne /

---

in the afternoon

popodne

поподне

/ **pɒ**pɒdne /

---

in the evening

uveče

увече

/ ʊvetʃe /

---

at night

noću

ноћу

/ nɒtjʊ /

---

afternoon

podne

подне

/ pɒdne /

---

annual

godišnje

годишње

/ gɒdɪʃnje /

---

calendar

kalendar

календар

/ kʌlendʌr /

---

daytime

dan

дан

/ dʌn /

decade

dekada

декада

/ dekʌdʌ /

---

evening

veče

вече

/ **ve**tʃe /

---

hour

sat

сат

/ sʌt /

---

midnight

ponoć

поноћ

/ **pɒ**nɒtj /

---

minute

minut

минут

/ **mɪ**nʊt /

---

morning

jutro

јутро

/ **jʊ**trɒ /

---

month

mesec

месец

/ **me**sets /

---

night

noć

ноћ

/ nɒtj /

---

night-time

noću

ноћу

/ **nɒ**tjʊ /

---

noon

podne

подне

/ **pɒ**dne /

---

now

sada

сада

/ **s**ʌdʌ /

---

o'clock

sat

сат

/ sʌt /

past

prošlost

прошлост

/ **prʊ**ʃlɒst /

present

sadašnjost

садашњост

/ sʌ**dʌ**ʃnɒst /

second

sekunda

секунда

/ se**kʊ**ndʌ /

sunrise

izlazak sunca

излазак сунца

/ ɪzlʌzʌk **sʊ**ntsʌ /

sunset

zalazak sunca

залазак сунца

/ **z**ʌlʌzʌk **sʊ**ntsʌ /

today

danas

данас

/ **d**ʌnʌs /

tonight

večeras

вечерас

/ vetʃerʌs /

tomorrow

sutra

сутра

/ sʊtrʌ /

watch

sat

сат

/ sʌt /

week

nedelja

недеља

/ nedeljʌ /

year

godina

година

/ gɒdɪnʌ /

yesterday

juče

јуче

/ jʊtʃe /

Months of the Year
Meseci u godini
Месеци у години

January

januar

јануар

/ **j**ʌnʊʌr /

February

februar

фебруар

/ **fe**brʊʌr /

March

mart

март

/ **m**ʌrt /

April

april

април

/ ʌprɪl /

May

maj

мај

/ mʌj /

June

jun

јун

/ jʊn /

July

jul

јул

/ jʊl /

August

avgust

август

/ ʌvgʊst /

September

septembar

септембар

/ septembʌr /

October

oktobar

октобар

/ ɒktɒbʌr /

November

novembar

новембар

/ nɒvembʌr /

December

decembar

децембар

/ de**ts**embʌr /

Days of the Week
Dani u sedmici
Дани у седмици

Monday

ponedeljak

понедељак

/ pɒ**ne**deljʌk /

Tuesday

utorak

уторак

/ ʊtɒrʌk /

Wednesday

sreda

среда

/ **sre**dʌ /

Thursday

četvrtak

четвртак

/ tʃetv**r**tʌk /

Friday

petak

петак

/ petʌk /

Saturday

subota

субота

/ sʊbɒtʌ /

Sunday

nedelja

недеља

/ nedeljʌ /

Seasons
Godišnja doba
Годишња доба

winter

zima

зима

/ zɪmʌ /

spring

proleće

пролеће

/ prɒletje /

summer

leto

лето

/ **le**tɒ /

---

fall/autumn

jesen

јесен

/ **je**sen /

Numbers
Brojevi

Бројеви

One (1)

jedan

један

/ **je**dʌn /

Two (2)

dva

два

/ dvʌ /

Three (3)

tri

три

/ trɪ /

Four (4)

četiri

четири

/ tʃetɪrɪ /

Five (5)

pet

пет

/ pet /

Six (6)

šest

шест

/ ʃest /

Seven (7)

sedam

седам

/ sedʌm /

Eight (8)

osam

осам

/ ɒsʌm /

Nine (9)

devet

девет

/ devet /

Ten (10)

deset

десет

/ **de**set /

Eleven (11)

jedanaest

једанаест

/ je**d**ʌnʌest /

Twelve (12)

dvanaest

дванаест

/ **dv**ʌnʌest /

Twenty (20)

dvadeset

двадесет

/ **dv**ʌdeset /

Fifty (50)

pedeset

педесет

/ pe**de**set /

Hundred (100)

sto

сто

/ stɒ /

Thousand (1000)

hiljadu

хиљаду

/ **hɪ**ljʌdʊ /

Ten Thousand (10,000)

deset hiljada

десет хиљада

/ **de**set **hɪ**ljʌdʌ /

One Hundred Thousand (100,000)

sto hiljada

сто хиљада

/ stɒ **hɪ**ljʌdʌ /

Million (1,000,000)

milion

милион

/ mɪ**lɪ**ɒn /

Billion (1,000,000,000)

milijarda

милијарда

/ mɪlɪ**j**ʌrdʌ /

Ordinal Numbers
Redni brojevi
Редни бројеви

first

prvi

први

/ prvɪ /

second

drugi

други

/ **drʊg**ɪ /

third

treći

трећи

/ **tre**tjɪ /

fourth

četvrti

четврти

/ **tʃe**tvtrtɪ /

fifth

peti

пети

/ **pe**tɪ /

sixth

šesti

шести

/ ʃestɪ /

---

seventh

sedmi

седми

/ sedmɪ /

---

eighth

osmi

осми

/ ɒsmɪ /

---

ninth

deveti

девети

/ devetɪ /

---

tenth

deseti

десети

/ desetɪ /

---

eleventh

jedanaesti

једанаести

/ jedʌnʌestɪ /

twelfth

dvanaesti

дванаести

/ dvʌnʌestɪ /

thirteenth

trinaesti

тринаести

/ trɪnʌestɪ /

twentieth

dvadeseti

двадесети

/ dvʌdesetɪ /

twenty-first

dvadeset prvi

двадесет први

/ dvʌdeset prvɪ /

hundredth

stoti

стоти

/ stɒtɪ /

thousandth

hiljaditi

хиљадити

/ hɪljʌdɪtɪ /

millionth

milioniti

милионити

/ mɪlɪɒnɪtɪ /

billionth

milijarditi

милијардити

/ mɪlɪjʌrdɪtɪ /

Geometric Shapes
Geometrijski oblici
Геометријски облици

angle

ugao

угао

/ ʊgʌɒ /

circle

krug

круг

/ krʊg /

cone

kupa

купа

/ kʊpʌ /

cube

kocka

коцка

/ **kɒ**tskʌ /

cylinder

cilindar

цилиндар

/ **tsɪ**lɪndʌr /

heart

srce

срце

/ srts**e** /

heptagon

sedmougao

седмоугао

/ **se**dmɒʊɡʌɒ /

hexagon

šestougao

шестоугао

/ **ʃe**stɒʊɡʌɒ /

line

linija

линија

/ **lɪ**nɪjʌ /

octagon

osmougao

осмоугао

/ ɒsmɒʊɡʌɒ /

---

oval

oval - ovoid

овал - овоид

/ ɒvʌl / - / ɒvɒɪd /

---

parallel lines

paralelne linije

паралелне линије

/ pʌrʌlelne lɪnɪje /

---

pentagon

petougao

петоугао

/ petɒʊɡʌɒ /

---

perpendicular lines

okomite linije

окомителиније

/ ɒkɒmɪtelɪnɪje /

---

polygon

mnogougao

многоугао

/ mnɒɡɒʊɡʌɒ /

pyramid

piramida

пирамида

/ pɪrʌmɪdʌ /

rectangle

pravougaonik

правоугаоник

/ prʌʊgʌɒnɪk /

rhombus

romb

ромб

/ rɒmb /

square

kvadrat

квадрат

/ kvʌdrʌt /

star

zvezda

звезда

/ zvezdʌ /

trapezoid

trapez

трапез

/ trʌpez /

triangle

trougao

троугао

/ **tr**ʊgʌɒ /

---

vortex

vrtlog

вртлог

/ **vr**tlɒg /

Colors
Boje
Боје

beige

bež

беж

/ beʒ /

---

black

crna

црна

/ **ts**rnʌ /

---

blue

plava

плава

/ **pl**ʌvʌ /

---

brown

braon

браон

/ **br**ʌɒn /

---

fuchsia

fuksija

фуксија

/ **f**ʊksɪjʌ /

---

gray

siva

сива

/ **s**ɪvʌ /

---

green

zelena

зелена

/ **ze**lenʌ /

---

indigo

modra

модра

/ **m**ɒdrʌ /

---

maroon

kestenjasta

кестењаста

/ **ke**stenjʌstʌ /

navy blue

tamnoplava

тамноплава

/ tʌmnɒplʌvʌ /

orange

narandžasta

наранџаста

/ nʌrʌndʒʌstʌ /

pink

roze

розе

/ rɒze /

purple

ljubičasta

љубичаста

/ ljʊbɪtʃʌstʌ /

red

crvena

црвена

/ tsrvenʌ /

silver

srebrna

сребрна

/ srebrnʌ /

tan

žuto-mrka

жуто-мрка

/ ʒʊtɒ - mrkʌ /

---

teal

modrozelena/tamno-tirkizna

модрозелена/тамно-тиркизна

/ mɒdrɒzelenʌ/tʌmnɒ - tɪrkɪznʌ /

---

turquoise

tirkizna

тиркизна

/ tɪrkɪznʌ /

---

violet

ljubičasta

љубичаста

/ ljʊbɪtʃʌstʌ /

---

white

bela

бела

/ belʌ /

---

yellow

žuta

жута

/ ʒʊtʌ /

Related Verbs
Srodni glagoli
Сродни глаголи

to add

dodati

додати

/ dɒdʌtɪ /

to change

promeniti

променити

/ prɒmenɪtɪ /

to check

proveriti

проверити

/ prɒverɪtɪ /

to color

obojiti

обојити

/ ɒbɒjɪtɪ /

to count

izbrojati

избројати

/ izbrɒjʌtɪ /

to divide

podeliti

поделити

/ pɒdelɪtɪ /

---

to figure

shvatiti

схватити

/ shvʌtɪtɪ /

---

to fill

napuniti

напунити

/ nʌpʊnɪtɪ /

---

to guess

pogoditi

погодити

/ pɒgɒdɪtɪ /

---

to measure

izmeriti

измерити

/ izmerɪtɪ /

---

to multiply

pomnožiti

помножити

/ pɒmnɒʒɪtɪ /

---

to subtract

oduzeti

одузети

/ ɒdʊzetɪ /

---

to take

uzeti

узети

/ ʊzetɪ /

---

to tell time

reći vreme

pећи време

/ **re**tjɪ **vre**me /

---

to verify

potvrditi

потврдити

/ pɒt**vr**dɪtɪ /

---

to watch

gledati

гледати

/ **gle**datɪ /

TEXT 1 – English original Orginalni Tekst na engleskom jeziku

Michael is a **ten** year old boy who lives in Georgia. His family owns a **twenty acre** farm; he has **two** brothers and **three** sisters. Michael loves to work on his family's farm. He and his brothers wake up at **6:00 in the morning** every day. His favorite thing to do is ride his

brown and **white** horse around the **perimeter** of the farm to check the fencing for damage. Even if there is only a **centimeter** of damaged wood, Michael must repair it. He also has to **measure** the **height** and **width** of the fence. He takes this job very seriously, so he doesn't want to miss a thing. Michael especially loves working on the farm in **autumn** because they sell more than **one thousand orange** pumpkins during the **month** of **October!** People from all over the state travel for **miles** to buy their pumpkins. Some of their pumpkins **weigh** as much as **one hundred pounds!** In the **winter**, his family sells Christmas trees. He loves helping other families find the perfect tree, whether it is **four feet**, **seven feet**, or even **nine feet tall**! In **December**, his family sells a **dozen green** trees a **day**, this keeps Michael very busy. In the **spring**, his family prepares the crops for the **summer** and **autumn** harvest. Because **spring** is such a busy **time** in school, each of the siblings take turns with special projects on the farm during the **week**; Michael's is the **first** day of the week, **Monday;** Henry's is the **second** day, **Tuesday**; Alan's is the **third** day, **Wednesday**; Sally's is the **fourth** day, **Thursday**; and Ann's is the **fifth** day, **Friday**. Little Ella is still too young for chores, but she loves to **measure** the **height** of the blooming **red** and **yellow** flowers with her **small ruler**. She is a **miniature** version of their mom. She cannot wait to grow up and help around the farm. During **summer**, Michael spends most of his **time** helping his mom cook. It is so hot outside, especially in **July** and **August**; he decided he needed a fun indoor activity. While cooking, he is learning how to convert different types of **measures**, like how many **teaspoons** are in a **tablespoon** and how many **cups** are in a **gallon**; he is also learning to add a **dash** here and **sprinkle** a **little** there to make the recipe just right. Mom knows cooking is a good skill to learn, but she also knows he will be learning these **measurements** in school this **September**.

TEXT – Serbian Latin Alphabet TEKST- Srpski jezik, latinično pismo

Majkl je **desetogodišnji** dečak koji živi u Džordžiji. Njegova porodica poseduje farmu od **dvadeset jutara**; on ima **dva** brata i **tri** sestre. Majkl voli da radi na svojoj porodičnoj farmi. On i njegova braća se bude svakog dana u **6 sati ujutru**. On najviše voli da jaše svog **braon-belog** konja oko **perimetra** svoje farme da proveri ima li oštećenja ograde. Čak i ako ima samo **centimetar** oštećenog drveta, Majkl mora to da popravi. On takođe mora da **izmeri visinu i širinu** ograde. On ovaj posao shvata veoma ozbiljno, tako da ne želi da mu ništa promakne. Majkl posebno voli da radi na farmi na **jesen** jer oni prodaju više **od sto hiljada narandžastih bundeva** tokom **meseca oktobra**! Ljudi iz cele države putuju **miljama** da kupe njihove bundeve. Neke od bundeva **teže** do **sto funti**! **Zimi**, njegova porodica prodaje božićne jelke. On voli da pomaže drugim porodicama da pronađu savršeno drvo, bez obzira da li je visoko **četiri stope**, **sedam stopa**, ili **devet stopa**! U **decembru**, njegova porodica prodaje **tuce zelenih** stabala **dnevno**, zato je Majkl veoma zauzet. U **proleće**, njegova porodica priprema useve za **letnju i jesenju** žetvu. Zato što je **proleće** veoma **naporno vreme** u školi, svaki član porodice se menja u posebnim zadacima na farmi u toku **nedelje**; Majkl je **prvog** dana u nedelji, **ponedeljkom**; Henri je **drugog** dana, **utorkom**, Alan je **trećeg** dana, **sredom**; Sali je **četvrtog** dana, **četvrtkom**; Ana je **petog** dana, **petkom**. Mala Ela je još uvek mala za poslove, ali voli da svojim **minijaturnim lenjirom meri visinu crvenih** i **žutih** cvetova u cvatu. Ona je **minijaturna** verzija svoje mame. Ona jedva čeka da poraste i pomaže na farmi. Tokom **leta**, Majkl većinu **vremena** provodi tako što pomaže svojoj majci u kuvanju. Napolju je veoma toplo, posebno u **julu i avgustu**; on je odlučio da mu je potrebna interesantna aktivnost unutra. Tokom kuvanja, on uči kako da pretvori različite vrste **mernih jedinica**, kao na primer koliko se **kašičica** nalazi u **kašiki**, a koliko **šolja** se nalazi u **galonu**; on takođe uči da ovde doda **malo i naspe** malo onde da bi recept bio odgovarajući. Mama zna da je dobra vežba naučiti kuvanje, ali ona takođe zna da će on učiti o ovim **mernim jedinicama** u **septembru** u školi.

TEXT – Serbian Cyrillic Alphabet TEKST- Srpski jezik, ćirilićno pismo

Мајкл је **десетогодишњи** дечак који живи у Џорџији. Његова породица поседује фарму од **двадесет јутара**; он има **два** брата и **три** сестре. Мајкл воли да ради на својој породичној фарми. Он и његова браћа се буде сваког дана у **6 сати ујутру**. Он највише воли да јаше свог **браон-белог** коња око **периметра** своје фарме да провери има ли оштећења ограде. Чак и ако има само **центиметар** оштећеног дрвета, Мајкл мора то да поправи. Он такође мора да **измери висину** и **ширину** ограде. Он овај посао схвата веома озбиљно, тако да не жели да му ништа промакне. Мајкл посебно воли да ради на фарми на **јесен** јер они продају више од **сто хиљада наранџастих бундева** током **месеца октобра**! Људи из целе државе путују **миљама** да купе њихове бундеве. Неке од бундева **теже** до **сто фунти**! Зими, његова породица продаје божићне јелке. Он воли да помаже другим породицама да пронађу савршено дрво, без обзира да ли је високо **четири стопе**, **седам стопа**, или **девет стопа**! У **децембру**, његова породица продаје **туце зелених** стабала **дневно**, зато је Мајкл веома заузет. У **пролеће**, његова породица припрема усеве за **летњу** и **јесењу** жетву. Зато што је **пролеће** веома **напорно време** у школи, сваки члан породице се мења у посебним задацима на фарми у току **недеље**; Мајкл је **првог** дана у недељи, **понедељком**; Хенри је **другог** дана, **уторком**, Алан је **трећег** дана, **средом**; Сали је **четвртог** дана, **четвртком**; Ана је **петог** дана, **петком**. Мала Ела је још увек мала за послове, али воли да својим **минијатурним лењиром мери висину црвених** и **жутих** цветова у цвату. Она је **минијатурна** верзија своје маме. Она једва чека да порасте и помаже на фарми. Током **лета**, Мајкл већину **времена** проводи тако што помаже својој мајци у кувању. Напољу је веома топло, посебно у **јулу** и **августу**; он је одлучио да му је потребна интересантна активност унутра. Током кувања, он учи како да претвори различите врсте **мерних јединица**, као на пример колико се **кашичица** налази у **кашики**, а колико **шоља** се налази у **галону**; он такође учи да овде **дода** мало и **наспе** мало онде да би рецепт био одговарајући. Мама зна да је добра вежба научити кување, али она такође зна да ће он учити о овим **мерним јединицама** у **септембру** у школи.

2) **Weather**
Vreme
Време

First Line - Vocabulary Item
Second Line - Serbian Latin
Third Line - Serbian Cyrillic
Fourth Line - Serbian Pronunciation

---

air
vazduh
ваздух
/ vʌzdʊh /

---

air pollution
zagađenje vazduha
загађење ваздуха
/ zʌgʌ**dje**nje vʌzdʊhʌ /

---

atmosphere
atmosfera
атмосфера
/ ʌtmɒsferʌ /

---

avalanche
lavina
лавина
/ **l**ʌvɪnʌ /

---

barometer

barometar

барометар

/ bʌrɒmetʌr /

---

barometric pressure

barometarski pritisak

барометарски притисак

/ bʌrɒmetʌrskɪ prɪtɪsʌk /

---

blizzard

mećava

мећава

/ metjʌvʌ /

---

breeze

povetarac

поветарац

/ pɒvetʌrats /

---

climate

klima

клима

/ klɪmʌ /

---

cloud

oblak

облак

/ ɒblʌk /

---

cold

hladno

хладно

/ **hl**ʌdnɒ /

---

cold front

hladan talas

хладан талас

/ **hl**ʌdʌn **t**ʌlʌs/

---

condensation

kondenzacija

кондензација

/ kɒndenzʌtsɪjʌ /

---

cool

svež

свеж

/ sve**ʒ** /

---

cyclone

ciklon

циклон

/ **ts**ɪklɒn /

---

degree

stepen

степен

/ **ste**pen /

depression

depresija

депресија

/ depresɪjʌ /

dew

rosa

роса

/ rɒsʌ /

dew point

tačka rose

тачка росе

/ tatʃkʌ rɒse /

downpour

pljusak

пљусак

/ pljʊsʌk /

drift

nanos

нанос

/ nʌnɒs /

drizzle

rominjati

роминьати

/ rɒmɪnjʌtɪ /

drought

suša

суша

/ **sʊ**ʃɒ /

dry

suvo

суво

/ **sʊ**vɒ /

dust devil

vetroviti vihor

ветровити вихор

/ vetrɒvɪtɪ **vɪ**hɒr /

duststorm

peščana oluja

пешчана олуја

/ **pe**ʃtʃʌnʌ ɒlʊjʌ /

easterly wind

istočni vetar

источни ветар

/ ɪstɒtʃnɪ **ve**tʌr /

evaporation

isparavanje

испаравање

/ ɪspʌrʌvʌnje /

eye of the storm

oko oluje

око олује

/ ɒkɒ ɒlʊje /

---

fair

lepo

лепо

/ lepɒ /

---

fall

padavine

падавине

/ pʌdʌvɪbe /

---

flash flood

bujica

бујица

/ bʊjcʌ /

---

flood

poplava

поплава

/ pɒplʌvʌ /

---

flood stage

nivo poplave

ниво поплаве

/ nɪvɒ pɒplʌve /

flurries (snow)

nalet (snega)

налет (снега)

/ nʌlet (snegʌ) /

---

fog

magla

магла

/ mʌglʌ /

---

forecast

prognoza

прогноза

/ prɒgnɒzʌ /

---

freeze

zamrzlina

замрзлина

/ zʌmrzlɪnʌ /

---

freezing rain

ledena kiša

ледена киша

/ ledenʌ kɪʃʌ /

---

front (cold/hot)

front (topao/hladan)

фронт (топао/хладан)

/ frɒnt (tɒpʌɒ/hlʌdʌn) /

frost

mraz

мраз

/ mrʌz /

---

funnel cloud

levkasti oblak

левкасти облак

/ levkʌstɪ ɒblʌk /

---

global warming

globalno otopljavanje

глобално отопљавање

/ glɒbʌlnɒ ɒtɒpljʌvʌnje /

---

gust of wind

nalet vetra

налет ветра

/ nʌlet vetrʌ /

---

hail

grad

град

/ grʌd /

---

haze

izmaglica

измаглица

/ ɪzmaglɪcʌ /

heat

vrelina

врелина

/ vrelɪnʌ /

---

heat index

indeks vreline

индекс врелине

/ ɪndeks vrelɪne /

---

heat wave

vreli talas

врели талас

/ **vre**lɪ **t**ʌlʌs /

---

high

visoko

високо

/ **vɪ**sɒkɒ /

---

humid

vlažan

влажан

/ vlʌʒʌn /

---

humidity

vlažnost

влажност

/ vlʌʒnɒst /

hurricane

uragan

ураган

/ ʊrʌgʌn /

ice

led

лед

/ lɛd /

ice crystals

ledeni kristali

ледени кристали

/ lɛdɛnɪ krɪstʌlɪ /

ice storm

ledena oluja

ледена олуја

/ lɛdɛnʌ ɒlʊjʌ /

icicle

ledenica

леденица

/ lɛdɛnɪtsʌ /

jet stream

mlazna struja

млазна струја

/ mlʌznʌ strʊjʌ/

landfall

odron

одрон

/ ɒdrɒn /

lightning

munja

муња

/ mʊnja /

low

nizak

низак

/ nɪzʌk /

low pressure system

sistem niskog pritiska

систем ниског притиска

/ sɪstem nɪskɒg prɪtɪskʌ /

meteorologist

meteorolog

метеоролог

/ meteɒrɒlɒg /

meteorology

meteorologija

метеорологија

/ meteɒrɒlɒgɪjʌ /

microburst

blago horizontalno strujanje vazduha

благо хоризонтално струјање ваздуха

/ blʌgɒ hɒrɪzɒntʌlnɒ strujʌnje vʌzduhʌ /

mist

izmaglica

измаглица

/ ɪzmʌglɪtsʌ /

moisture

vlažnost

влажност

/ vlʌʒnɒst /

monsoon

monsun

монсун

/ mɒnsʊn /

muggy

sparan

спаран

/ spʌrʌn /

nor'easter

severo-istočnjak

северо-источњак

/ severɒ-ɪstɒtʃnjʌk /

normal

normalan

нормалан

/ nɒrmʌlʌn /

---

outlook

izgled

изглед

/ ɪzgled /

---

overcast

tmuran

тмуран

/ tmʊrʌn /

---

ozone

ozon

озон

/ ɒzɒn /

---

partly cloudy

delimično oblačno

делимично облачно

/ delɪmɪtʃnɒ ɒblʌtʃnɒ /

---

polar

polarni

поларни

/ pɒlʌrnɪ /

pollutant

zagađivač

загађивач

/ zʌgʌ**djɪ**vʌtʃ /

---

precipitation

padavine

падавине

/ **pʌ**dʌvɪne /

---

pressure

pritisak

притисак

/ **prɪ**tɪsʌk /

---

radar

radar

радар

/ **rʌ**dʌr /

---

radiation

radijacija

радијација

/ rʌdɪ**jʌ**tsɪjʌ /

---

rain

kiša

киша

/ **kɪ**ʃʌ /

---

rainbow

duga

дуга

/ dʊgʌ /

rain gauge

kišomer

кишомер

/ kɪʃɒmer /

relative humidity

relativna vlažnost

релативна влажност

/ relʌtɪvnʌ vlʌʒnɒst /

sandstorm

peščana oluja

пешчана олуја

/ peʃtʃʌnʌ ɒlʊjʌ /

season

godišnje doba

годишње доба

/ gɒdɪʃnje dɒbʌ /

shower

pljusak

пљусак

/ pljʊsʌk /

sky

nebo

небо

/ **ne**bɒ /

---

sleet

susnežica

суснежица

/ **sʊ**sneʒɪtsʌ /

---

slush

ljapavica

љапавица

/ **lj**ʌpʌvɪtsʌ /

---

smog

smog

смог

/ smɒg /

---

smoke

dim

дим

/ dɪm /

---

snow

sneg

снег

/ sn**e**g /

snowfall

padanje snega

падање снега

/ pʌdʌnje snegʌ /

snowflake

pahuljica

пахуљица

/ pʌhʊljɪtsʌ /

snow flurry

nalet snega

налет снега

/ nʌlet snegʌ /

snow shower

snežni pljusak

снежни пљусак

/ sneʒnɪ pljʊsʌk /

snowstorm

snežna oluja

снежна олуја

/ sneʒnʌ ɒlʊjʌ /

spring

proleće

пролеће

/ prɒletje /

storm

oluja

олуја

/ ɒlʊjʌ /

---

storm surge

olujni talas

олујни талас

/ ɒlʊjnɪ tʌlʌs /

---

stratosphere

stratosfera

стратосфера

/ strʌtɒsferʌ /

---

summer

leto

лето

/ letɒ /

---

sunrise

izlazak sunca

излазак сунца

/ ɪzlʌzʌk sʊntsʌ /

---

sunset

zalazak sunca

залазак сунца

/ zʌlʌzʌk sʊntsʌ /

supercell

super ćelija

супер ћелија

/ sʊper tjelɪjʌ /

surge

veliki talas

велики талас

/ velɪkɪ tʌlʌs /

swell

nadut

надут

/ nʌdʊt /

temperature

temperatura

температура

/ temperʌtʊrʌ /

thaw

topljenje

топљење

/ tʊpljenje /

thermal

termalni

термални

/ termʌlnɪ /

thermometer

termometar

термометар

/ **ter**mɒmetʌr /

---

thunder

grmljavina

грмљавина

/ **grm**ljʌvɪnʌ /

---

thunderstorm

oluja

олуја

/ ɒlʊjʌ /

---

tornado

tornado

торнадо

/ tɒr**nʌ**dɒ /

---

trace

malo

мало

/ **m**ʌlɒ /

---

tropical

tropski

тропски

/ **tr**ɒpskɪ /

---

tropical depression

tropska depresija

тропска депресија

/ **trɒ**pskʌ **de**presɪjʌ /

---

tropical storm

tropska oluja

тропска олуја

/ **trɒ**pskʌ ɒlʊjʌ /

---

turbulence

turbulencija

турбуленција

/ **tʊr**bʊlentsɪjʌ /

---

twister

tornado

торнадо

/ **tɒr**nʌdɒ /

---

typhoon

tajfun

тајфун

/ **tʌj**fʊn /

---

unstable

nestabilno

нестабилно

/ **ne**stʌbɪlnɒ /

visibility

vidljivost

видљивост

/ **vɪ**dljɪvɒst /

vortex

vir

вир

/ vɪr /

warm

toplo

топло

/ **tʊ**plɒ /

warning

upozorenje

упозорење

/ ʊpɒzʊrenje /

watch

gledati

гледати

/ **gle**dʌtɪ /

weather

vreme

време

/ **vre**me /

weather pattern

vremenski obrazac

временски образац

/ **vre**menskɪ ɒbrʌzʌts /

weather report

vremenski izveštaj

временски извештај

/ **vre**menskɪ ɪzveʃtʌj /

weather satellite

vremenski satelit

временски сателит

/ **vre**menskɪ sʌtelɪt /

westerly wind

zapadni vetar

западни ветар

/ **zʌ**pʌdnɪ **ve**tʌr /

whirlwind

vihor

вихор

/ **vɪ**hɒr /

wind

vetar

ветар

/ **ve**tʌr /

wind chill

osećaj ugodnosti

осећај угодности

/ ɒsetjʌj ʊgɒdnɒstɪ /

---

winter

zima

зима

/ zɪmʌ /

Related verbs
Srodni glagoli
Сродни глаголи

to blow

duvati

дувати

/ dʊvʌtɪ /

---

to clear up

raščistiti

рашчистити

/ rʌʃtʃɪstɪtɪ /

---

to cool down

zahladneti

захладнети

/ zʌhlʌdnetɪ /

to drizzle

rominjati

ромињати

/ rɒmɪnjʌtɪ /

to feel

osećati

осећати

/ ɒsetjʌtɪ /

to forecast

predvideti

предвидети

/ **pre**dvɪdetɪ /

to hail

padati (grad)

падати (град)

/ **p**ʌdʌtɪ (**gr**ʌd) /

to rain

padati (kiša)

падати (киша)

/ **p**ʌdʌtɪ (**k**ɪʃʌ) /

to report

izvestiti

известити

/ ɪz**ve**stɪtɪ /

to shine

sijati (sunce)

сијати (сунце)

/ sɪjʌtɪ(sʊntse) /

---

to snow

padati (sneg)

падати (снег)

/ pʌdʌtɪ (sneg) /

---

to storm

burno duvati

бурно дувати

/ bʊrnɒ dʊvʌtɪ /

---

to warm up

otopliti

отоплити

/ ɒtɒplɪtɪ /

---

to watch

gledati

гледати

/ gledʌtɪ /

TEXT – English original Orginalni Tekst na engleskom jeziku

Heather loves the **seasons** and **weather**. She dreams of one day becoming a **meteorologist** so she can share her love with everyone. She is currently attending school to study the **weather** and how it works. She is learning that each of the four **seasons** brings its own

weather patterns to the world. She is amazed at how the **seasons** affect the **weather**. The **seasons** vary throughout the world, but here in America, where Heather lives, there are four distinct **seasons**, and each of them brings something different to our world. In **winter**, the **temperature** is **cold** and the ground is white with **snow**. The **wind** gets so **cold** up on the mountaintop that the **wind chill** is below zero **degrees**. Sometimes, the **wind** blows with such force that it causes an **avalanche** of **snow** on the mountain. When the **air** is this **cold**, you are likely to wake up with **frost** on your car. In the **spring**, things begin to **heat** up. The **temperature** begins to **warm** up a bit, making the **snow** on the ground **thaw** out. The flowers begin to bloom and the trees begin to grow leaves. **Spring** often brings **rain**; sometimes the **rain** is so heavy, it causes **flash floods**. A common sighting in spring is a beautiful **rainbow** after the **rain**. The **temperature** is **hot** in the **summer**. The **temperatures** begin to rise and the **heat index** goes up causing a **heat wave**. There is not much **precipitation** in **summer**; however, occasionally the **clouds** bring a **thunderstorm**. The **rain** usually does not last long in **summer**, but the **thunder** and **lightning** can be dangerous. Every time there is a **thunderstorm**, Heather will watch the **weather report** to see if they will issue a **watch** or a **warning**. After **summer**, **fall** brings the start of **cool temperatures**. The leaves on the trees begin to fall, preparing the tree for the **winter**. In the coastal regions, **hurricanes** become a problem in the **fall**. This is a dangerous, yet exciting time in the world of **meteorology**. The **seasons** have a huge effect on **weather**; however the biggest changes in **weather** and the most dangerous events, such as **tsunamis**, **tornados**, and **storms**, occur during the change in **seasons**. The **unstable** and ever-changing **temperatures** affect the **barometric pressure** in a way that causes these types of events. While dangerous, they are exciting to someone like Heather who studies the **weather**. Heather's goal is to one day help educate and warn people in advance when these events are likely to occur.

TEXT – Serbian Latin Alphabet TEKST- Srpski jezik, latinično pismo

Heder voli **godišnja doba** i **vreme**. Ona mašta o tome da jednoga dana postane **meteorolog** tako da može da deli svoju ljubav sa svima. Ona trenutno ide u školu da proučava **vreme** i kako ono funkcioniše. Ona uči da svako od četiri **godišnja doba** donosi svoje **vremenske obrasce** svetu. Zadivljena je time kako **godišnja doba** utiču na **vreme**. **Godišnja doba** variraju širom sveta, ali ovde u Americi, gde Heder živi, postoje četiri različita **godišnja doba**, i svako od njih donosi nešto drugačije našem svetu. **Zimi**, **temperatura** je **hladna** a zemlja je bela od **snega**. **Vetar** je toliko **hladan** na vrhovima planina tako da je **temperatura vetra** ispod nula **stepeni**. Ponekad, **vetar** duva sa takvom jačinom da stvara **lavine snega** na planini. Kada je **vazduh ovoliko** hladan, postoji verovatnoća da ćete se probuditi sa **mrazom** na svojim kolima. U **proleće**, stvari počinju da se **zagrevaju**. **Temperatura** počinje polako da se **povećava**, i zato se **sneg** na zemlji **topi**. Cveće počinje da cveta i na drveću počinje da raste lišće. **Proleće** često donosi **kišu**; ponekad je **kiša** toliko jaka da stvara **bujice**. Česta pojava u proleće je lepa **duga** posle **kiše**. **Temperatura** je **topla leti**. **Temperature** počinju da rastu i **indeks toplote** se povećava i stvara **toplotni talas**. Nema mnogo **padavina leti**; međutim, ponekad **oblaci** donose **oluju**. **Leti**, **kiša** obično ne traje dugo, ali **grmljavina** i **munja** mogu da budu opasni. Ponekad se javljaju **oluje**, Heder gleda **vremenski izveštaj** da vidi da li će izdati **upozorenje**. Nakon **leta**, **jesen** donosi početak **hladnih temperatura**. Lišće na drveću počinje da opada, i priprema drveće za **zimu**. U priobalnim delovima, **hurikani** postaju problem na **jesen**. Ovo je opasno, ali uzbudljivo vreme u svetu **meteorologije**. **Godišnja doba** imaju veliki uticaj na **vreme**, međutim najveće promene u **vremenu** i najopasniji događaji, kao što su **cunami**, **tornada** i **oluje**, se dešavaju prilikom promene **godišnjih doba**. **Nestabilne** i uvek promenljive **temperature** utiču na **barometarski pritisak** na način koji izaziva ove vrste događaja. Iako opasni, oni su zanimljivi nekome kao što je Heder koja proučava

vreme. Hederin cilj je da jednog dana obrazuje i unapred upozori ljude kada postoji verovatnoća da se ovi događaji odigraju.

TEXT – Serbian Cyrilic Alphabet TEKST- Srpski jezik, ćirilično pismo

Хедер воли **годишња доба** и **време**. Она машта о томе да једнога дана постане **метеоролог** тако да може да дели своју љубав са свима. Она тренутно иде у школу да проучава **време** и како оно функционише. Она учи да свако од четири **годишња доба**доноси своје **временске обрасце** свету. Задивљена је тиме како **годишња доба** утичу на **време**. **Годишња доба** варирају широм света, али овде у Америци, где Хедер живи, постоје четири различита **годишња доба**, и свако од њих доноси нешто другачије нашем свету. **Зими, температура** је **хладна** а земља је бела од **снега**. **Ветар** је толико **хладан** на врховима планина тако да је **температура ветра** испод нула **степени**. Понекад, **ветар** дува са таквом јачином да ствара **лавине снега** на планини. Када је **ваздух** оволико **хладан**, постоји вероватноћа да ћете се пробудити са **мразом** на својим колима. У **пролеће**, ствари почињу да се **загревају**. **Температура** почиње полако да се **повећава**, и зато се **снег** на земљи **топи**. Цвеће почиње да цвета и на дрвећу почиње да расте лишће. **Пролеће** често доноси **кишу**; понекад је **киша** толико јака да ствара **бујице**. Честа појава у **пролеће** је лепа **дуга** после **кише**. **Температура** је **топла лети**. **Температуре** почињу да **расту** и **индекс топлоте** се повећава и ствара **топлотни талас**. Нема много **падавина лети**; међутим, понекад **облаци** доносе **олују**. **Лети, киша** обично не траје дуго, али **грмљавина** и **муња** могу да буду опасни. Понекад се јављају **олује**, Хедер гледа **временски извештај** да види да ли ће издати **упозорење**. Након **лета, јесен** доноси почетак **хладних температура**. Лишће на дрвећу почиње да опада, и припрема дрвеће за **зиму**. У приобалним деловима, **хурикани** постају проблем на **јесен**. Ово је опасно, али узбудљиво време у свету **метеорологије**. **Годишња доба** имају велики утицај на **време**, међутим највеће промене у

времену и најопаснији догађаји, као што су **цунами**, **торнада** и **олује**, се дешавају приликом промене **годишњих доба.·** **Нестабилне** и увек променљиве **температуре** утичу на **барометарски притисак** на начин који изазива ове врсте догађаја. Иако опасни, они су занимљиви некоме као што је Хедер која проучава **време**. Хедерин циљ је да једног дана образује и унапред упозори људе када постоји вероватноћа да се ови догађаји одиграју.

3) People
Ljudi
Људи

First Line - Vocabulary Item
Second Line - Serbian Latin
Third Line - Serbian Cyrillic
Fourth Line - Serbian Pronunciation

---

athlete
sportista
спортиста
/ spɒrtɪstʌ /

---

baby
beba
беба
/ bebʌ /

---

boy
dečak
дечак
/ detʃʌk /

---

boyfriend
dečko
дечко
/ detʃkɒ /

---

brother

brat

брат

/ brʌt /

---

brother-in-law

zet

зет

/ zet /

---

businessman

biznismen

бизнисмен

/ **bɪz**nɪsmen /

---

candidate

kandidat

кандидат

/ kʌn**dɪ**dʌt /

---

child/children

dete/deca

дете/деца

/ **de**te/**de**tsʌ /

---

coach

trener

тренер

/ **tre**ner /

---

cousin

rođak

рођак

/ **rɒ**djʌk /

customer

mušterija

муштерија

/ mʊ**šte**rıjʌ /

daughter

ćerka

ћерка

/ **tje**rkʌ /

daughter-in-law

snaja

снаја

/ **sn**ʌjʌ /

driver

vozač

возач

/ **vɒ**zʌtʃ /

family

porodica

породица

/ **pɒ**rɒdıtsʌ /

farmer

farmer

фармер

/ fʌrmer /

father/dad

otac/tata

отац/тата

/ ɒtʌts/tʌtʌ /

father-in-law

svekar

свекар

/ svekʌr /

female

žensko

женско

/ ʒenskɒ /

friend

prijatelj

пријатељ

/ prijʌtelj /

girl

devojčica

девојчица

/ devɒjtʃitsʌ /

girlfriend

devojka

девојка

/ deᴠɒjkʌ /

---

godparents

kumovi

кумови

/ kʊmɒvɪ /

---

grandchildren

unuci

унуци

/ ʊnʊtsɪ /

---

granddaughter

unuka

унука

/ ʊnʊkʌ /

---

grandfather

deda

деда

/ dedʌ /

---

grandmother

baba

баба

/ bʌbʌ /

---

grandparents

deda i baba

деда и баба

/ de dʌ ɪ bʌbʌ /

---

grandson

unuk

унук

/ ʊnʊk /

---

husband

suprug

супруг

/ sʊprʊg /

---

instructor

instruktor

инструктор

/ ɪnstrʊktɒr /

---

kid

dete

дете

/ dete /

---

king

kralj

краљ

/ krʌlj /

---

male

muško

мушко

/ **mʊ**ʃkɒ /

man

čovek

човек

/ **tʃɒ**vek /

mother/mom

majka/mama

мајка/мама

/ **mʌ**jkʌ/**mʌ**mʌ /

mother-in-law

svekrva

свекрва

/ **sve**krvʌ /

nephew

nećak / sestrić / bratanac

нећак / сестрић / братанац

/ **ne**tjʌk / **se**strɪtj / brʌtʌnʌts /

niece

nećaka / sestrična / bratanica

нећака / сестрична / братаница

/ **ne**tjʌkʌ / **se**strɪtʃnʌ / brʌtʌnɪtsʌ /

parent

roditelj

родитељ

/ **rɒ**dɪtelj /

---

people

ljudi

људи

/ **ljʊ**dɪ /

---

princess

princeza

принцеза

/ prɪn**tse**zʌ /

---

queen

kraljica

краљица

/ **krʌ**ljɪtsʌ /

---

rock star

rok zvezda

рок звезда

/ rɒk **zve**zdʌ /

---

sister

sestra

сестра

/ **se**strʌ /

---

sister-in-law

zaova

заова

/ zɑɒvʌ /

son

sin

син

/ sɪn /

son-in-law

zet

зет

/ zet /

student

student

студент

/ stʊdent /

teenager

tinejdžer

тинејџер

/ tɪnejdʒer /

tourist

turista

туриста

/ tʊrɪstʌ /

wife

supruga

супруга

/ **sʊ**prʊgʌ /

---

woman

žena

жена

/ **ʒ**enʌ /

---

youth

mladi

млади

/ **ml**ʌdɪ /

Characteristics
Karakteristike
Карактеристике

attractive

atraktivan

атрактиван

/ ʌtrʌktɪvʌn /

---

bald

ćelav

ћелав

/ **tje**lʌv /

---

beard

brada

брада

/ **br**ʌdʌ /

beautiful

lep

леп

/ l**e**p /

black hair

crna kosa

црна коса

/ **ts**rnʌ kɒsʌ /

blind

slep

слеп

/ sl**e**p /

blond

plav

плав

/ pl**ʌ**v /

blue eyes

plave oči

плаве очи

/ **pl**ʌve ɒtʃɪ /

brown eyes

braon oči

браон очи

/ brʌɒn ɒtʃɪ /

---

brown hair

braon kosa

браон коса

/ brʌɒn kɒsʌ /

---

brunette

brineta

бринета

/ brɪnetʌ /

---

curly hair

kovrdžava kosa

коврџава коса

/ kɒvrdʒʌvʌ kɒsʌ /

---

dark

taman

таман

/ tʌmʌn /

---

deaf

gluv

глув

/ glʊv /

---

divorced

razveden

разведен

/ rʌzveden /

---

elderly

star

стар

/ stʌr /

---

fair (skin)

svetla (koža)

светла (кожа)

/ svetlʌ (kɒʒʌ) /

---

fat

debeo

дебео

/ debeɒ /

---

gray hair

seda kosa

седа коса

/ sedʌ kɒsʌ /

---

green eyes

zelene oči

зелене очи

/ zelene ɒtʃɪ /

handsome

zgodan

згодан

/ **zgɒ**dʌn /

---

hazel eyes

oči boje lešnika

очи боје лешника

/ **ɒ**tʃɪ **bɒ**je leʃnɪkʌ /

---

heavyset

krupne građe

крупне грађе

/ **krʊ**pne **grʌ**dje /

---

light brown

svetlo braon

светло браон

/ **svet**lɒ **brʌ**ɒn /

---

long hair

duga kosa

дуга коса

/ **dʊg**ʌ **kɒ**sʌ /

---

married

oženjen/udata

ожењен/удата

/ **ɒ**ʒenjen/**ʊd**ʌtʌ /

mustache

brkovi

бркови

/ **br**kɒvɪ /

---

old

star

стар

/ stʌr /

---

olive

maslinast

маслинаст

/ **m**ʌslɪnʌst /

---

overweight

pretežak

претежак

/ **pre**teʒʌk /

---

pale

bled

блед

/ bl**e**d /

---

petite

sitan

ситан

/ **sɪ**tʌn /

---

plump

punačak

пуначак

/ pʊnʌtʃʌk /

---

pregnant

trudna

трудна

/ trʊdnʌ /

---

red head

crvena kosa

црвена коса

/ tsrvenʌ kɒsʌ /

---

short

nizak

низак

/ nɪzʌk /

---

short hair

kratka kosa

кратка коса

/ krʌtkʌ kɒsʌ /

---

skinny

žgoljav

жгољав

/ʒgɒljʌv /

slim

vitak

витак

/ vɪtʌk /

stocky

zdepast

здепаст

/ zdepʌst /

straight hair

prava kosa

права коса

/ prʌvʌ kɒsʌ /

tall

visok

висок

/ vɪsɒk /

tanned

preplanuo

преплануо

/ preplʌnʊɒ /

thin

mršav

мршав

/ mrʃʌv /

wavy hair

talasasta kosa

таласаста коса

/ tʌlʌsʌstʌ kɒsʌ /

---

well built

krupan

крупан

/ krʊpʌn/

---

white

beo

бео

/ beɒ /

---

young

mlad

млад

/ mlʌd /

Stages of Life

Životne etape

Животне етапе

adolescence

adolescencija

адолесценција

/ ʌdɒlestsentsɪjʌ /

adult

odrasla osoba

одрасла особа

/ ɒdrʌslʌ ɒsɒbʌ /

---

anniversary

godišnjica

годишњица

/ gɒdɪʃnjɪtsʌ /

---

birth

rođenje

рођење

/ rɒdjenje /

---

death

smrt

смрт

/ smrt /

---

divorce

razvod

развод

/ rʌzvɒd /

---

elderly

stariji

старији

/ stʌrɪjɪ /

graduation

matura

матура

/ mʌtʊrʌ /

---

infant

odojče

одојче

/ ɒdɒjtʃe /

---

marriage

brak

брак

/ brʌk /

---

middle aged

srednjih godina

средњих година

/ **sre**dnjɪh **gɒ**dɪnʌ /

---

newborn

novorođenče

новорођенче

/ nɒvɒrɒdjentʃe /

---

preschooler

pred-školarac

пред-школарац

/ **pre**d-ʃkɒlʌrʌts /

---

preteen

mlađi od 13 godina

млађи од 13 година

/ **mlʌ**djɪ ɒd **trɪ**naest **gɒ**dɪnʌ /

senior citizen

stariji građanin

старији грађанин

/ st**ʌ**rɪjɪ gr**ʌ**dj**ʌ**nɪn /

teenager

tinejdžer

тинејџер

/ **tɪ**nejdʒer /

toddler

dete

дете

/ **de**te /

tween

dete između 10-12 godina starosti

дете између 10-12 година старости

/ **de**te izmedjʊ 10-12 **gɒ**dɪnʌ st**ʌ**rɒstɪ/

young adult

mlada osoba

млада особа

/ **mlʌ**dʌ ɒsɒb**ʌ** /

youth

mladost

младост

/ **mlʌ**dɒst /

Religion

Religija

Религија

AtheistAgnostic

ateista/agnostik

атеиста/агностик

/ ʌte**ɪ**stʌ/ʌg**nɒ**stɪk /

Baha'i

bahai

бахаи

/ bʌ**hʌ**ɪ /

Buddhist

budista

будиста

/ **bʊ**dɪstʌ /

Christian

hrišćanin

хришћанин

/ **hrɪ**ʃtjʌnɪn /

Hindu

hindu

хинду

/ **hɪ**ndʊ /

Jewish

jevrejin

јеврејин

/ **je**vrejɪn /

Muslim

musliman

муслиман

/ mʊslɪmʌn /

Sikh

sik

сик

/ sɪk /

Work

Posao

Посао

accountant

računovođa

рачуновођа

/ rʌtʃʊnɒvɒdjʌ /

actor

glumac

глумац

/ glʊmʌts /

---

associate

saradnik

сарадник

/ sʌrʌdnɪk /

---

astronaut

astronaut

астронаут

/ ʌstrɒnʌʊt /

---

banker

bankar

банкар

/ bʌnkʌr /

---

butcher

mesar

месар

/ mesʌr /

---

carpenter

stolar

столар

/ stʊlʌr /

chef

kuvar

кувар

/ kʊvʌr /

clerk

službenik

службеник

/ slʊʒbenɪk /

composer

kompozitor

композитор

/ kɒmpɒzɪtɒr /

custodian

domar

домар

/ dɒmʌr /

dentist

zubar

зубар

/ zʊbʌr /

doctor

doktor

доктор

/ dɒktɒr /

electrician

električar

електричар

/ elektrɪtʃʌr /

executive

direktor

директор

/ dɪrektɒr /

farmer

farmer

фармер

/ fʌrmer /

fireman

vatrogasac

ватрогасац

/ vʌtrɒgʌsʌts /

handyman

majstor

мајстор

/ mʌjstɒr /

judge

sudija

судија

/ sʊdɪjʌ /

landscaper

pejzažni arhitekta

пејзажни архитекта

/ **pe**jzʌʒnɪ ʌrhɪtektʌ /

lawyer

advokat

адвокат

/ ʌdvɒkʌt /

librarian

bibliotekar

библиотекар

/ **bɪ**blɪɒtekʌr /

manager

menadžer

менаџер

menʌdžer

model

model

модел

/ **m**ɒdel /

notary

beležnik

бележник

/ **be**leʒnɪk /

nurse

medicinska sestra

медицинска сестра

/ meditsɪnskʌ sestrʌ /

---

optician

optičar

оптичар

/ ɒptɪtʃʌr /

---

pharmacist

farmaceut

фармацеут

/ fʌrmʌtseʊt /

---

pilot

pilot

пилот

/ pɪlɒt /

---

policeman

policajac

полицајац

/ pɒlɪtsʌjʌts /

---

preacher

propovednik

проповедник

/ prɒpɒvednɪk /

---

president

predsednik

председник

/ **pre**dsednɪk /

representative

predstavnik

представник

/ **pre**dstʌvnɪk /

scientist

naučnik

научник

/ **n**ʌʊtʃnɪk /

secretary

sekretar

секретар

/ **se**kretʌr /

singer

pevač

певач

/ **pe**vʌtʃ /

soldier

vojnik

војник

/ **v**ɒjnɪk /

teacher

nastavnik

наставник

/ nʌstʌvnɪk /

---

technician

tehničar

техничар

/ tehnɪtʃʌr /

---

treasurer

blagajnik

благајник

/ blʌgʌjnɪk /

---

writer

pisac

писац

/ pɪsʌts /

---

zoologist

zoolog

зоолог

/ zɒɒlɒg /

Related Verbs
Srodni glagoli
Сродни глаголи

to deliver

isporučiti

испоручити

/ ɪspɒ**rut**ʃɪtɪ /

to enjoy

uživati

уживати

/ ʊ**ʒɪ**vʌti /

to grow

porasti

порасти

/ **pɒ**rʌstɪ /

to laugh

smejati se

смејати се

/ **sme**jʌtɪ se /

to love

voleti

волети

/ **vɒ**letɪ /

to make

napraviti

направити

/ nʌprʌvɪtɪ /

to manage

upravljati

управљати

/ ʊprʌvljʌtɪ /

to repair

popraviti

поправити

/ pɒprʌvɪtɪ /

to serve

služiti

служити

/ slʊʒɪtɪ /

to sing

pevati

певати

/ pevʌtɪ /

to smile

smejati se

смејати се

/ smejʌtɪ se /

to talk

pričati

причати

/ **prɪ**tʃʌtɪ /

---

to think

misliti

мислити

/ **mɪ**slɪtɪ /

---

to work

raditi

радити

/ **rʌ**dɪtɪ /

---

to work at

raditi u

радити у

/ **rʌ**dɪtɪ ʊ /

---

to work for

raditi za

радити за

/ **rʌ**dɪtɪ zʌ /

---

to work on

raditi na

радити на

/ **rʌ**dɪtɪ nʌ /

---

to worship

obožavati

обожавати

/ ɒbɒˈʒʌvʌti /

---

to write

pisati

писати

/ ˈpɪsʌtɪ /

TEXT – English original Orginalni Tekst na engleskom jeziku

John is a successful **pilot** and **businessman**. This came as no surprise to any of his **family** and **friends**, but his start in life wasn't an easy one. When he was just a **baby**, John spent a lot of time seeing **doctors** for a rare condition he was born with. As an **infant**, he was very sick and required the care of a **nurse** all the time. While he was in the hospital, everyone came to visit him; **aunts**, **uncles**, **cousins**, and of course his **grandparents**. Finally, he got well and he was able to live a normal, healthy life. Because of all he had been through, his **parents** knew he would be a successful **man**. As a **toddler**, he and his **grandfather** loved to watch planes fly over his house. John's **grandfather** told his **grandson** that he could be anything he wanted when he grew up. He was such a curious **child**, but never lost his love of planes, he even dreamed of being an **astronaut**. As he grew older, he really excelled in math and science class, his **teachers** were amazed and his **mom** and **dad** were so proud of him. He was the top **student** in his class when he graduated high school. He was a **tall**, **handsome young man** with **black hair** and **blue eyes**. He was also very talented on the basketball court; his **coach** thought he was a fine **youth** as well. He was just a **teenager** when he finished college and became a **pilot**, finally getting to live his lifelong dream. One day there was an accident that forced John into the hospital for quite some time, there he met a young **woman** named Rachel, and she was a **nurse.** John quickly recovered under the care of his **girlfriend**, but he was never able to fly again. He did however become a flight school **instructor** where he was able to teach other people how to fly. It wasn't long that John and Rachel because **husband** and **wife.** They had two lovely **children,** one **boy** and one **girl.** Jill is quite the **singer**; everything is a microphone to this aspiring **rock star.** She is the cutest little **princess** you have ever seen! But Little Johnny Junior is following in his **father's** footsteps because he dreams of being a **pilot**, just like his **daddy. Father, son,** and **grandson** all love to spend quiet Sunday afternoons watching the planes go by. John knows that one day his **son** will be able to fly planes just like he did. While this thought scares him a little because of the accident, he is very proud of his **son** for his passion for flying. Maybe one day he will be a **student** in his **father's** flight school. In all of his successes, John's **family** is the achievement he is most proud of.

TEXT – Serbian Latin Alphabet TEKST- Srpski jezik, latinično pismo

Džon je uspešan **pilot** i **biznismen**. Ovo nije bilo iznenađenje za nikoga od njegove **porodice** i **prijatelja**, ali njegov početak u životu nije bio lak. Kada je bio **beba**, Džon je morao često kod **doktora** zbog retke bolesti s kojom je rođen. On je bio veoma bolestan kao **beba** i bilo je potrebno da se **medicinska sestra** stalno brine o njemu. Dok je bio u bolnici, svi su mu došli u posetu: **tetke, teče, rođaci**, i naravno njegovi **baba i deda**. Na kraju je ozdravio i bio je u stanju da živi normalan, zdrav život. Zbog svega što je prošao, njegovi **roditelji** su znali da će biti uspešan **čovek**. Kao **malo dete**, njegov **deda** i on su voleli da gledaju avione kako lete iznad njihove kuće. Džonov **deda** je rekao svom **unuku** da može da bude sve što poželi kada poraste. On je bio veoma radoznalo **dete**, ali nikada nije prestao da voli avione, čak je sanjao da bude i **astronaut**. Kako je postajao stariji, briljirao je na časovima matematike i prirodnih nauka, njegovi **nastavnici** su bili oduševljeni a njegova **mama** i njegov **tata** su bili ponosni na njega. Bio je najbolji đak u **generaciji** kada je završio srednju školu. Bio je **visok, zgodan mladi čovek** sa **crnom kosom** i **plavim očima**. Bio je takođe talentovan za košarku; njegov **trener** je takođe mislio da je dobar **mladić**. Bio je samo **tinejdžer** kada je završio fakultet i postao **pilot**, konačno je živeo svoj dugogodišnji san. Jednog dana se desila nesreća koja je primorala Džona da bude u bolnici neko vreme, tamo je upoznao mladu **ženu** po imenu Rejčel, a ona je bila **medicinska sestra**. Džon se ubrzo oporavio pod brigom svoje **devojke**, ali nikada više nije mogao ponovo da leti. Međutim, on je postao **instruktor** letenja u školi, gde je mogao da uči druge ljude kako da lete. Nije prošlo puno vremena a Džon i Rejčel su postali **muž i žena**. Imali su dvoje divne **dece**, jednog **dečaka** i jednu **devojčicu**. Džil je dobra **pevačica**; sve je mikrofon ovoj **rok zvezdi** u usponu. Ona je najslađa mala **princeza** koju ste ikada videli! Ali mali Džon Junior ide **očevim** stopama jer on sanja o tome da bude **pilot**, kao i njegov **tata**. **Otac, sin,** i **unuk** vole da provode tiho nedeljno popodne gledajući avione kako prolaze. Džon zna da će njegov **sin** biti u stanju da upravlja avionima jednog dana kao i on. Dok ga ova misao pomalo plaši zbog nesreće, on je veoma ponosan na svog **sina** zbog njegove strasti za letenjem. Možda će jednog dana biti **učenik** u **očevoj** školi letenja. Od svih njegovih uspeha, Džonova **porodica** je postignuće na koje je on najponosniji.

TEXT – Serbian Cyrilic Alphabet TEKST- Srpski jezik, ćirilično pismo

Џон је успешан **пилот** и **бизнисмен**. Ово није било изненађење за никога од његове **породице** и **пријатеља**, али његов почетак у животу није био лак. Када је био **беба**, Џон је морао често код **доктора** због ретке болести с којом је рођен. Он је био веома болестан као **беба** и било је потребно да се **медицинска сестра** стално брине о њему. Док је био у болници, сви су му дошли у посету: **тетке, тече, рођаци,** и наравно његови **баба и деда**. На крају је оздравио и био је у стању да живи нормалан, здрав живот. Због свега што је прошао, његови родитељи су знали да ће бити успешан **човек**. Као **мало дете**, његов **деда** и он су волели да гледају авионе како лете изнад њихове куће. Џонов

деда је рекао свом **унуку** да може да буде све што пожели када порасте. Он је био веома радознало **дете**, али никада није престао да воли авионе, чак је сањао да буде и **астронаут**. Како је постајао старији, бриљирао је на часовима математике и природних наука, његови **наставници** су били одушевљени а његова **мама** и његов **тата** су били поносни на њега. Био је најбољи ђак у **генерацији** када је завршио средњу школу. Био је **висок, згодан млади човек** са **црном косом** и **плавим очима**. Био је такође талентован за кошарку; његов **тренер** је такође мислио да је **добар младић**. Био је само **тинејџер** када је завршио факултет и постао **пилот**, коначно је живео свој дугогодишњи сан. Једног дана се десила несрећа која је приморала Џона да буде у болници неко време, тамо је упознао **младу жену** по имену Рејчел, а она је била **медицинска сестра**. Џон се убрзо опоравио под бригом своје **девојке**, али никада више није могао поново да лети. Међутим, он је постао **инструктор** летења у школи, где је могао да учи друге људе како да лете. Није прошло пуно времена а Џон и Рејчел су постали **муж** и **жена**. Имали су двоје дивне **деце**, једног **дечака** и једну **девојчицу**. Џил је добра **певачица**; све је микрофон овој **рок звезди** у успону. Она је најслађа мала **принцеза** коју сте икада видели! Али мали Џон Јуниор иде **очевим** стопама јер он сања о томе да буде **пилот**, као и његов **тата**. **Отац, син**, и **унук** воле да проводе тихо недељно поподне гледајући авионе како пролазе. Џон зна да ће његов **син** бити у стању да управља авионима једног дана као и он. Док га ова мисао помало плаши због несреће, он је веома поносан на свог **сина** због његове страсти за летењем. Можда ће једног дана бити **ученик** у **очевој** школи летења. Од свих његових успеха, Џонова **породица** је постигнуће на које је он најпоноснији.

4) Parts of the Body
Delovi tela
Делови тела

First Line - Vocabulary Item
Second Line - Serbian Latin
Third Line - Serbian Cyrillic
Fourth Line - Serbian Pronunciation

---

ankle
zglob
зглоб
/ zglɒb /

---

arm
ruka
рука
/ rʊkʌ /

---

back
leđa
леђа
/ ledjʌ /

---

beard
brada
брада
/ brʌdʌ /

---

belly

stomak

стомак

/ **stɒ**mʌk /

---

blood

krv

крв

/ **krv** /

---

body

telo

тело

/ **tel**ɒ /

---

bone

kost

кост

/ **kɒ**st /

---

brain

mozak

мозак

/ **mɒ**zʌk /

---

breast

grudi

груди

/ **grʊ**dɪ /

---

buttocks

zadnjica

задњица

/ zʌdnjɪtsʌ /

calf

list (noge)

лист (ноге)

/ lɪst (nɒge) /

cheek

obraz

образ

/ ɒbrʌz /

chest

grudi

груди

/ grʊdɪ /

chin

brada

брада

/ brʌdʌ /

ear

uvo

уво

/ ʊvɒ /

elbow

lakat

лакат

/ **lʌ**kʌt /

---

eye

oko

око

/ **ɒ**kɒ /

---

eyebrow

obrva

обрва

/ **ɒ**brvʌ /

---

eyelash

trepavica

трепавица

/ **tre**pʌvɪtsʌ /

---

face

lice

лице

/ **lɪ**tse /

---

finger

prst

прст

/ **p**rst /

---

finger nail

nokat (na prstu ruke)

нокат (на прсту руке)

/ **nɒ**kʌt (na **pr**stʊ **rʊ**ke) /

---

fist

pesnica

песница

/ **pe**snıʌ /

---

flesh

telo

тело

/ **te**lɒ /

---

foot/feet

stopalo/stopala

стопало/стопала

/ **stɒ**pʌlɒ/**stɒ**pʌlʌ /

---

forearm

podlaktica

подлактица

/ **pɒ**dlʌktıtsʌ /

---

forehead

čelo

чело

/ **tʃe**lɒ /

---

hair

kosa

коса

/ **kɒ**sʌ /

---

hand

ruka

рука

/ **rʊ**kʌ /

---

head

glava

глава

/ **gl**ʌvʌ /

---

heart

srce

срце

/ **sr**tse /

---

heel

peta

пета

/ **pe**tʌ /

---

hip

kuk

кук

/ **k**ʊk /

---

jaw

vilica

вилица

/ vɪlɪtsʌ /

---

knee

koleno

колено

/ kɒlenɒ /

---

leg

noga

нога

/ nɒgʌ /

---

lips

usne

усне

/ ʊsne /

---

moustache

brkovi

бркови

/ brkɒvɪ /

---

mouth

usta

уста

/ ʊstʌ /

muscle

mišić

мишић

/ **mɪ**ʃitj /

nail

nokat

нокат

/ **nɒ**kʌt /

neck

vrat

врат

/ vrʌt /

nose

nos

нос

/ nɒs /

nostril

nozdrva

ноздрва

/ **nɒ**zdrvʌ /

palm

dlan

длан

/ dlʌn /

shin

golenjača

голењача

/ gʊlenjʌtʃʌ /

shoulder

rame

раме

/ rʌme /

skin

koža

кожа

/ kʊʒʌ /

spine

kičma

кичма

/ kɪtʃmʌ /

stomach

stomak

стомак

/ stʊmʌk /

teeth/tooth

zubi/zub

зуби/зуб

/ zʊbɪ/zʊb /

thigh

butina

бутина

/ **bʊ**tɪnʌ /

---

throat

grlo

грло

/ **gr**lɒ /

---

thumb

palac

палац

/ **p**ʌlʌts /

---

toe

prst na nozi

прст на нози

/ **pr**st na **n**ɒzɪ /

---

toenail

nokat (na nožnom prstu)

нокат (на ножном прсту)

/ **n**ɒkʌt /

---

tongue

jezik

језик

/ **je**zɪk /

---

underarm

pazuh

пазух

/ **pʌ**zʊh /

---

waist

struk

струк

/ strʊk /

---

wrist

zglob

зглоб

/ zglɒb /

Related Verbs
Srodni glagoli
Сродни глаголи

to exercise

vežbati

вежбати

/ **ve**ʒbʌtɪ /

---

to feel

osećati

осећати

/ ɒ**se**tjʌtɪ /

to hear

slušati

слушати

/ sluʃʌtɪ /

---

to see

videti

видети

/ vɪdetɪ /

---

to smell

pomirisati

помирисати

/ pɒmɪrɪsʌtɪ /

---

to taste

probati

пробати

/ prɒbʌtɪ /

---

to touch

dodirnuti

додирнути

/ dɒdɪrnʊtɪ /

TEXT – English original Orginalni Tekst na engleskom jeziku

One day an alien crash landed on planet Earth. He was very confused and didn't know where he was. As he explored this undiscovered world, he happened along a little boy named David. David was eight years old and wasn't scared at all; after all, he knew there were aliens and he was happy to finally meet one. The alien had a large **head** and funny pointing **ears;** and he moved in a curious way with six **legs**! The alien was so confused when he saw the boy, so he asked David, "Why do you look so funny?" David laughed and told him all humans look like this. David has a good **heart** and wanted to make sure the alien was familiar with the people of Earth, so he told him all about how we use our body parts. "Let me tell you all about these funny parts", replied David. "On top of my body is my **head**; we have two **eyes** to see; two **ears** to hear; a **nose** to smell; and a **mouth** to talk and eat." The alien was surprised because he had all of these parts, but they looked much different. "Well then," said the alien, "what are those things you are standing on and why are there only two of them? David said, "These are **legs**, we just put one in front of the other and it makes us walk or run." The alien was amazed that the human could walk with only two **legs,** after all, he had six **legs** and he needed them all to get around! "What are those things that are dangling off your upper **legs**?" asked the alien. "Oh, these? They are called **fingers** and they are attached to my **hands** and **arms**. Look! Aren't they neat? I can wiggle them, tickle with them, I even use them to pick things up. They really come in handy for lots of different things." The alien really wanted a set of those fingers, and then to find out there are **toes** on the end of the **legs**... wow! He just had to have some! The alien wanted to know more, so he continued, "What is that stuff sticking up on the top of your **head**?" David replied, "That is called **hair**. It grows really fast, even after I cut it off, it just grows back out!! Adult humans have **hair** on other parts of their bodies; l**egs, arms, face,** even their **toes**!" "Why don't you have **hair** on those parts?" asked the alien. David told him that he would not grow **hair** on those parts until he grows up. The alien was satisfied with David's explanation of the human body parts and decided it was time to return home. David was sad to see him go, but so excited to tell his friends all about his encounter with such a curious alien.

TEXT – Serbian Latin Alphabet TEKST- Srpski jezik, latinično pismo

Jednog dana svemirac se srušio na Zemlju. On je bio vrlo zbunjen i nije znao gde je. Dok je istraživao ovaj neotkriveni svet, sreo je dečaka po imenu Dejvid. Dejvid je imao osam godina i uopšte nije bio uplašen; uostalom, znao je da postoje svemirci i bio je srećan da konačno upozna jednog. Svemirac je imao veliku **glavu** i smešne šiljate **uši**; a čudno se kretao sa svojih šest **nogu**! Svemirac je bio zbunjen kada je video dečaka, pa je pitao Dejvida, "Zašto izgledaš tako smešno?" Dejvid se nasmejao i rekao mu da svi ljudi tako izgledaju. Dejavid ima dobro **srce** i želeo je da se uveri da je svemirac upoznat sa ljudima na Zemlji, pa mu je rekao sve o tome kako mi koristimo naše delove tela. "Dozvoli mi da ti kažem o ovim smešnim delovima" odgovorio je Dejvid. "Na vrhu mog tela je **glava**; imamo dva **oka** za vid; dva **uveta** za sluh; **nos** za miris; a **usta** za pričanje i jelo." Svemirac je bio iznenađen jer je on imao ove delove tela ali su izgledali mnogo drugačije. "Pa onda," rekao je svemirac "šta je to na čemu stojiš i zašto ih ima samo dve." Dejvid je rekao "Ovo su **noge**, mi stavljamo jednu ispred druge i tako hodamo ili trčimo." Svemirac je bio iznenađen da ljudi mogu da hodaju samo sa dve **noge**, ipak, on je imao šest **nogu** i sve su mu bile potrebne da se kreće! "Šta je to što ti visi na gornjim **nogama**? Oh, ovo? To se zove **prsti**, i spojeni su sa mojim **šakama** i **rukama**. Vidi! Zar nisu divni? Mogu da ih mrdam, da njima golicam, ja ih čak mogu koristiti da podižem stvari. Zaista su korisni za puno različitih stvari." Svemirac je stvarno želeo ovakve **prste**, a onda je otkrio da postoje **nožni prsti** na kraju **nogu**...vau! On prosto mora da ih ima! Svemirac je želeo da zna više pa je nastavio "Šta je ta stvar što stoji na vrhu tvoje **glave**?" Dejvid je odgovorio "To se zove **kosa**. Vrlo brzo raste, čak i kada je isečem, ona ponovo izraste!!! Odrasli ljudi imaju **dlake** na drugim delovima tela; **noge**, **ruke**, **lice** čak i na **nožnim prstima**!" "Zašto ti nemaš **dlake** na tim delovima?" upitao je svemirac. Dejvid mu je rekao da mu **dlake** neće izrasti na tim delovima dok ne poraste. Svemirac je bio zadovoljan Dejvidovim objašnjenjem delova ljudskog tela i odlučio je da je vreme da se vrati kući. Dejvid je bio tužan kada je video da odlazi, ali veoma uzbuđen da ispriča svojim prijateljima o svom susretu sa radoznalim svemircem.

TEXT – Serbian Cyrilic Alphabet TEKST- Srpski jezik, ćirilićno pismo

Једног дана свемирац се срушио на Земљу. Он је био врло збуњен и није знао где је. Док је истраживао овај неоткривени свет, срео је дечака по имену Дејвид. Дејвид је имао осам година и уопште није био уплашен; уосталом, знао је да постоје свемирци и био је срећан да коначно упозна једног. Свемирац је имао велику **главу** и смешне шиљате **уши**; а чудно се кретао са својих шест **ногу**! Свемирац је био збуњен када је видео дечака, па је питао Дејвида, "Зашто изгледаш тако смешно?" Дејвид се насмејао и рекао му да сви људи тако изгледају. Дејавид има добро **срце** и желео је да се увери да је свемирац упознат са људима на Земљи, па му је рекао све о томе како ми користимо наше делове тела. "Дозволи ми да ти кажем о овим смешним деловима" одговорио је Дејвид. "На врху мог тела је **глава**; имамо два **ока** за вид; два **увета** за слух; **нос** за мирис; а **уста** за причање и јело." Свемирац је био изненађен јер је он имао ове делове тела али су изгледали много другачије. "Па онда," рекао је свемирац "шта је то на чему стојиш и зашто их има само две." Дејвид је рекао "Ово су **ноге**, ми стављамо једну испред друге и тако ходамо или трчимо." Свемирац је био изненађен да људи могу да ходају само са две **ноге**, ипак, он је имао шест **ногу** и све су му биле потребне да се креће! "Шта је то што ти виси на горњим **ногама**? Ох, ово? То се зове **прсти**, и спојени су са мојим **шакама** и **рукама**. Види! Зар нису дивни? Могу да их мрдам, да њима голицам, ја их чак могу користити да подижем ствари. Заиста су корисни за пуно различитих ствари." Свемирац је стварно желео овакве **прсте**, а онда је открио да постоје **ножни прсти** на крају ногу...вау! Он просто мора да их има! Свемирац је желео да зна више па је наставио "Шта је та ствар што стоји на врху твоје **главе**?" Дејвид је одговорио "То се зове **коса**. Врло брзо расте, чак и када је исечем, она поново израсте!!! Одрасли људи имају **длаке** на другим деловима тела; **ноге, руке, лице** чак и на **ножним прстима**!” “Зашто ти немаш **длаке** на тим деловима?” упитао је свемирац. Дејвид му је рекао да му **длаке** неће израсти на тим деловима док не порасте. Свемирац је био задовољан Дејвидовим објашњењем делова људског тела и одлучио је да је време да се врати кући. Дејвид је био тужан када је видео да одлази, али веома узбуђен да исприча својим пријатељима о свом сусрету са радозналим свемирцем.

5) Animals
Životinje
Животиње

First Line - Vocabulary Item
Second Line - Serbian Latin
Third Line - Serbian Cyrillic
Fourth Line - Serbian Pronunciation

---

alligator
aligator
алигатор
/ ʌlɪgʌtɒr /

---

anteater
mravojed
мравојед
/ mrʌvɒjed /

---

antelope
antilopa
антилопа
/ ʌntɪlɒpʌ /

---

ape
majmun
мајмун
/ mʌjmʊn /

---

armadillo

oklopnik

оклопник

/ ɒklɒpnɪk /

---

baboon

babun

бабун

/ bʌbʊn /

---

bat

slepi miš

слепи миш

/ slepɪ mɪʃ /

---

bear

medved

медвед

/ medved /

---

beaver

dabar

дабар

/ dʌbʌr /

---

bison

bizon

бизон

/ bɪzɒn /

---

bobcat

ris

рис

/ rɪs /

---

camel

kamila

камила

/ kʌmɪlʌ /

---

caribou

karibu

карибу

/ kʌrɪbʊ /

---

cat

mačka

мачка

/ mʌtʃkʌ /

---

chameleon

kameleon

камелеон

/ kʌmeleɒn /

---

cheetah

gepard

гепард

/ gepʌrd /

---

chipmunk

veverica

веверица

/ **ve**verɪtsʌ /

---

cougar

kuguar

кугуар

/ **ku**guʌr /

---

cow

krava

крава

/ **kr**ʌvʌ /

---

coyote

kojot

којот

/ **kɒ**jɒt /

---

crocodile

krokodil

крокодил

/ krɒ**kɒ**dɪl /

---

deer

jelen

јелен

/ **je**len /

---

dinosaur

dinosaurus

диносаурус

/ dɪnɒsʌʊrʊs /

dog

pas

пас

/ pʌs /

donkey

magarac

магарац

/ mʌgʌrvts /

elephant

slon

слон

/ slɒn /

emu

emu

ему

/ emʊ /

ferret

omčica

омчица

/ ɒmtʃɪtsʌ /

fox

lisica

лисица

/ lɪsitsʌ /

frog

žaba

жаба

/ ʒʌbʌ /

gerbil

skočimiš

скочимиш

/ skɒtʃɪmɪʃ /

giraffe

žirafa

жирафа

/ ʒɪrʌfʌ /

goat

koza

коза

/ kɒzʌ /

gorilla

gorila

горила

/ gɒrɪlʌ /

groundhog

mrmot

мрмот

/ **mr**mɒt /

---

guinea pig

zamorče

заморче

/ **z**ʌmɒrtʃe /

---

hamster

hrčak

хрчак

/ **hr**tʃʌk /

---

hedgehog

jež

јеж

/ j**e**ʒ /

---

hippopotamus

nilski konj

нилски коњ

/ **nɪ**lskɪ kɒnj /

---

horse

konj

коњ

/ k**ɒ**nj /

---

iguana

iguana

игуана

/ ɪgʊʌnʌ /

kangaroo

kengur

кенгур

/ **ke**ngʊr /

lemur

lemur

лемур

/ **le**mʊr /

leopard

leopard

леопард

/ leɒpʌrd /

lion

lav

лав

/ lʌv /

lizard

gušter

гуштер

/ **gʊ**ʃter /

llama

lama

лама

/ lʌmʌ /

---

meerkat

merkat

меркат

/ **me**rkʌt /

---

mouse/mice

miš/miševi

миш/мишеви

/ mɪʃ/**mɪ**ʃevɪ /

---

mole

krtica

кртица

/ **kr**tɪtsʌ /

---

monkey

majmun

мајмун

/ **m**ʌjmʊn /

---

moose

los

лос

/ lɒs /

---

mouse

miš

миш

/ miʃ /

otter

vidra

видра

/ **vɪ**drʌ /

panda

panda

панда

/ **pʌ**ndʌ /

panther

panter

пантер

/ **pʌ**nter /

pig

svinja

свиња

/ **svɪ**nja /

platypus

kljunar

кљунар

/ **kljʊ**nʌr /

polar bear

polarni medved

поларни медвед

/ pɒlʌrnɪ **me**dved /

---

porcupine

bodljikavo prase

бодљикаво прасе

/ **bɒ**dljɪkʌvɒ **pr**ʌse /

---

rabbit

zec

зец

/ **ze**ts /

---

raccoon

rakun

ракун

/ **r**ʌkʊn /

---

rat

pacov

пацов

/ **p**ʌtsɒv /

---

rhinoceros

nosorog

носорог

/ **n**ɒsɒrɒg /

---

sheep

ovca

овца

/ ɒvtsʌ /

---

skunk

tvor

твор

/ tvɒr /

Birds
Ptice
Птице

---

robin

crvendać

црвендаћ

/ tsrvendʌtj /

---

chicken

kokoška

кокошка

/ kɒkɒʃkʌ /

---

crow

vrana

врана

/ vrʌnʌ /

dove

golubica

голубица

/ gɒlʊbɪtsʌ /

---

duck

patka

патка

/ pʌtkʌ /

---

eagle

orao

орао

/ ɒrʌɒ /

---

falcon

soko

соко

/ sɒkɒ /

---

flamingo

flamingo

фламинго

/ flʌmɪngɒ /

---

goose

guska

гуска

/ gʊskʌ /

---

hawk

jastreb

јастреб

/ jʌstreb /

hummingbird

kolibri

колибри

/ kɒlɪbrɪ /

ostrich

noj

нoj

/ nɒj /

owl

sova

сова

/ sɒvʌ /

parrot

papagaj

папагај

/ pʌpʌgʌj /

peacock

paun

паун

/ pʌʊn /

pelican

pelikan

пеликан

/ pelɪkʌn /

---

pheasant

fazan

фазан

/ fʌzʌn /

---

pigeon

golub

голуб

/ gɒlʊb /

---

canary

kanarinac

канаринац

/ kʌnʌrɪnʌts /

---

rooster

pevac

певац

/ pevʌts /

---

sparrow

vrabac

врабац

/ vrʌbʌts /

---

swan

labud

лабуд

/ lʌbʊd /

---

turkey

ćurka

ћурка

/ tjʊrkʌ /

Water/Ocean/Beach
Voda/Okean/Plaža
Вода/Океан/Плажа

bass

grgeč

гргеч

/ grgetʃ /

---

catfish

som

сом

/ sɒm /

---

clam

školjka

шкољка

/ ʃkɒljkʌ /

crab

kraba

краба

/ krʌbʌ /

goldfish

zlatna ribica

златна рибица

/ zlʌtna rɪbɪtsʌ /

jellyfish

meduza

медуза

/ medʊzʌ /

lobster

jastog

јастог

/ jʌstɒg /

mussel

dagnja

дагња

/ dʌgnjʌ/

oyster

ostriga

острига

/ ɒstrɪgʌ /

salmon

losos

лосос

/ lɒsɒs /

shark

ajkula

ајкула

/ ʌjkʊlʌ /

trout

pastrmka

пастрмка

/ pʌstrmkʌ /

tuna

tuna

туна

/ tʊnʌ /

whale

kit

кит

/ kɪt /

Insects
Insekti
Инсекти

ant

mrav

мрав

/ mrʌv /

---

bee

pčela

пчела

/ **ptʃe**lʌ /

---

beetle

buba

буба

/ **bʊ**bʌ /

---

butterfly

leptir

лептир

/ **le**ptɪr /

---

cockroach

bubašvaba

бубашваба

/ bʊbʌ**ʃvʌ**bʌ /

---

dragonfly

vilin konjic

вилин коњиц

/ vɪlɪn kɒnjɪts /

earthworm

kišna glista

кишна глиста

/ kɪʃnʌ glɪstʌ /

flea

buva

бува

/ bʊvʌ /

fly

muva

мува

/ mʊvʌ /

gnat

komarac

комарац

/ kɒmʌrʌts /

grasshopper

skakavac

скакавац

/ skʌkʌvʌts /

ladybug

bubamara

бубамара

/ bʊbʌmʌrʌ /

---

moth

moljac

мољац

/ mɒljʌts /

---

mosquito

komarac

комарац

/ kɒmʌrʌts /

---

spider

pauk

паук

/ pʌʊk /

---

wasp

osa

оса

/ ɒsʌ /

Related Verbs
Srodni glagoli
Сродни глаголи

to eat

jesti

јести

/ **je**stɪ /

---

to bark

lajati

лајати

/ **lʌ**jʌtɪ /

---

to chase

juriti

јурити

/ **jʊ**rɪtɪ /

---

to feed

hraniti

хранити

/ **hrʌ**nɪtɪ /

---

to hibernate

hibernirati

хибернирати

/ hɪber**nɪ**rʌtɪ /

---

to hunt

loviti

ловити

/ lɒvɪtɪ /

to move

kretati se

кретати се

/ kretʌtɪ se /

to perch

spustiti se

спустити се

/ spʊstɪtɪ se/

to prey

loviti

ловити

/ lɒvɪtɪ /

to run

trčati

трчати

/ trtʃʌtɪ /

to swim

plivati

пливати

/ plɪvʌtɪ /

to wag

mahati, gegati se

махати, гегати се

/ mʌhʌtɪ, gegʌtɪ se/

---

to walk

hodati

ходати

/ hɒdʌtɪ /

TEXT – English original Orginalni Tekst na engleskom jeziku

Sarah is a seven year old girl who loves to visit the zoo. Her mom takes her to the local zoo at least once a week to see her favorite animals. This is an account of her usual visit to the zoo: When they arrive, they must pass by the **flamingos** and boy do they smell! They are pretty to look at, but don't get too close! Sarah insists that they visit her favorite animal first, the **elephants**. She loves how big, yet gentle they are. They spend time watching the **elephants** move about their habitat and one time, she even got to see an **elephant** paint! Next, they visit the Birds' Nest exhibit. They have many different species of **birds** on display, including **sparrows, robins, peacocks, canaries, hummingbirds**, they even have an **eagle**! The **eagle** is so majestic; it is Sarah's favorite **bird**. Sometimes the **eagle**'s trainer will put on a show and Sarah just loves to see it spread its wings! After visiting the birds, Sarah likes to visit the mammal section of the zoo. They have **bears, tigers, lions, monkeys**, they even have **pandas**! One of the **pandas** had twin babies last year and Sarah has really enjoyed watching them grow up. After lunch, they visit the **reptile** house; there are lots of scaly looking animals there! The **alligators** are big and scary, but Sarah likes to watch from a distance. They also have **frogs** in lots of different colors; some are green, some are yellow and black, and some are blue! The best animals in the **reptile** house are the **snakes**. Some are stretched out long and some are coiled up taking a nap! They come in many different colors as well. Did you know that **snakes** eat **mice**? Sarah once got to see a **snake** eat its lunch, it was a little yucky to watch, but neat to see how a **snake** eats. After visiting the **reptiles**, Sarah and her mom go to see the **meerkats** and **warthogs**. They always make Sarah think of her favorite movie characters. The **meerkats** are silly little creatures and the **warthogs** just lay around in the mud all day! Sarah then goes to visit the tallest animal in the zoo, the **giraffe.** One day she even got to feed one! Its mouth is very weird to touch and it has a long tongue. One of the more popular sites at the zoo is the petting zoo. Sarah gets to brush the coat of **goats**, **sheep**, and even **pigs**! One last stop, to ride the train. While on the zoo train, Sarah gets to see lots of different animals, such as **kangaroos**, **ostriches**, **turtles**, and many more! Maybe one day, Sarah's mom can talk her into going to the aquarium instead of the zoo. Sarah would surely enjoy seeing **sharks**, **whales**, and **jellyfish**!

TEXT – Serbian Latin Alphabet TEKST- Srpski jezik, latinično pismo

Sara je sedmogodišnja devojčica koja voli da posećuje zoološki vrt. Njena majka je vodi u zoološki vrt makar jednom nedeljno da vidi svoje omiljene životinje. Ovo je prikaz njene tipične posete zoološkom vrtu: Kada stignu, moraju da prođu pored **flamingosa** a oni itekako smrde! Njih je lepo gledati, ali ne prilazite previše blizu. Sara insinstira da prvo posete njene omiljene životinje, **slonove**. Ona voli koliko su oni veliki a ipak nežni. One provode vreme gledajući **slonove** kako se kreću u svom staništu, a jednom je čak videla **slona** kako slika! Zatim, oni posećuju izložbu ptičijih gnezda. Na izložbi ima mnogo različitih vrsta **ptica**, uključujući **vrapce**, **crvendaće**, **paunove**, **kanarince**, **kolibrije**, oni čak imaju i **orla**! **Orao** je veoma veličanstven; to je Sarina omiljena **ptica**. Ponekad trener **orlova** priredi predstavu a Sara jednostavno voli da gleda kako on širi krila! Nakon posete **pticama**, Sara voli da posećuje deo zoološkog vrta sa **sisarima**. Oni imaju **medvede**, **tigrove**, **lavove**, **majmune**, oni čak imaju i **pande**! Jedna od **pandi** je prošle godine dobila blizance i Sara je vrlo volela da ih gleda kako rastu. Nakon ručka, oni posećuju deo sa **reptilima**: postoji mnoštvo životinja sa krljuštima tamo! **Aligatori** su veliki i strašni, ali Sara voli da ih gleda sa daljine. Imaju takođe i **žabe** u raznim bojama; neke su zelene, neke su žute i crne, a neke su plave! **Zmije** su najbolje životinje u odeljku sa **reptilima**. Neke su skroz ispružene a neke su sklupčane dok dremaju! One su takođe različitih boja. Da li ste znali da **zmije** jedu **miševe**? Sara je jednom gledala kako **zmija** jede svoj ručak, bilo je malo odvratno za gledanje, ali divno za videti kako **zmija** jede. Nakon posete **reptilima**, Sara i njena majka idu da vide **merkate i bradavičaste svinje**. Zbog njih Sara uvek pomisli na svoje omiljene likove iz filmova. **Merkati** su blesava mala stvorenja, a **bradavičaste svinje** samo leže unaokolo u blatu po ceo dan! Sara onda ide da poseti najvišuživotinju u zoološkom vrtu, **žirafu**. Jednom je čak i nahranila jednu! Usta su joj veoma čudna za dodirnuti i ima dugačak jezik. Jedno od popularnijih mesta u zoološkom vrtu je farma. Sara tu može češljati krzno **koze**, **ovce**, pa čak i **svinje**! Poslednja stanica je vožnja vozom. Dok je u vozu zoološkog vrta, Sara može da vidi mnoštvo različitih životinja kao što su **kenguri, nojevi, kornjače**, i mnoge druge! Možda će je jednog dana njena majka nagovoriti da posete **akvarijum** umesto zoološkog vrta. Sara bi svakako uživala da vidi **ajkule, kitove** i **meduze**!

TEXT – Serbian Cyrilic Alphabet TEKST- Srpski jezik, ćirilično pismo

Сара је седмогодишња девојчица која воли да посећује зоолошки врт. Њена мајка је води у зоолошки врт макар једном недељно да види своје омиљене животиње. Ово је приказ њене типичне посете зоолошком врту: Када стигну, морају да прођу поред **фламингоса** а они итекако смрде! Њих је лепо гледати, али не прилазите превише близу. Сара инсинстира да прво посете њене омиљене животиње, **слонове**. Она воли колико су они велики а ипак нежни. Оне проводе време гледајући **слонове** како се крећу у свом станишту, а једном је чак видела **слона** како слика! Затим, они посећују изложбу птичијих гнезда. На изложби има много различитих врста **птица**, укључујући **врапце, црвендаће, паунове, канаринце, колибрије,** они чак имају и **орла**! **Орао** је веома величанствен; то је Сарина омиљена **птица**. Понекад тренер **орлова** приреди представу а Сара једноставно воли да гледа како он шири крила! Након посете **птицама**, Сара воли да посећује део зоолошког врта са **сисарима**. Они имају **медведе, тигрове, лавове, мајмуне,** они чак имају и **панде**! Једна од **панди** је прошле године добила близанце и Сара је врло волела да их гледа како расту. Након ручка, они посећују део са **рептилима**: постоји мноштво животиња са крљуштима тамо! **Алигатори** су велики и страшни, али Сара воли да их гледа са даљине. Имају такође и **жабе** у разним бојама; неке су зелене, неке су жуте и црне, а неке су плаве! Змије су најбоље животиње у одељку са **рептилима**. Неке су скроз испружене а неке су склупчане док дремају! Оне су такође различитих боја. Да ли сте знали да **змије** једу **мишеве**? Сара је једном гледала како **змија** једе свој ручак, било је мало одвратно за гледање, али дивно за видети како **змија** једе. Након посете **рептилима**, Сара и њена мајка иду да виде **меркате** и **брадавичасте свиње**. Због њих Сара увек помисли на своје омиљене ликове из филмова. **Меркати** су блесава мала створења, а **брадавичасте свиње** само леже унаоколо у блату по цео дан! Сара онда иде да посети највишу животињу у зоолошком врту, **жирафу**. Једном је чак и нахранила једну! Уста су јој веома чудна за додирнути и има дугачак језик. Једно од популарнијих места у зоолошком врту је фарма. Сара ту може чешљати крзно **козе, овце**, па чак и **свиње**! Последња станица је вожња возом. Док је у возу зоолошког врта, Сара може да види мноштво различитих животиња као што су **кенгури, нојеви, корњаче,** и многе друге! Можда ће је једног дана њена мајка наговорити да посете **акваријум** уместо зоолошког врта. Сара би свакако уживала да види **ајкуле**, **китове** и медузе!

6) Plants and Trees
Biljke i drveće
Биљке и дрвеће

First Line - Vocabulary Item
Second Line - Serbian Latin
Third Line - Serbian Cyrillic
Fourth Line - Serbian Pronunciation

---

acacia
bagrem
багрем
/ **bʌ**grem /

---

acorn
žir
жир
/ ʒɪr /

---

annual
godišnji
годишњи
/ **gɒ**dɪʃnjɪ /

---

apple tree
jabuka
јабука
/ **jʌ**bʊkʌ /

---

bamboo

bambus

бамбус

/ **b**ʌmbʊs /

bark

kora

кора

/ **k**ɒrʌ /

bean

pasulj

пасуљ

/ **p**ʌsʊlj /

berry

bobica

бобица

/ **b**ɒbɪtsʌ /

birch

breza

бреза

/ **b**rezʌ /

blossom

cvet

цвет

/ tsvet /

branch

grana

грана

/ grʌnʌ /

brush

četka

четка

/ tʃetkʌ /

bud

pupoljak

пупољак

/ pʊpɒljʌk /

bulb

lukovica

луковица

/ lʊkɒvɪtsʌ /

bush

grm

грм

/ grm /

cabbage

kupus

купус

/ kʊpʊs /

cactus

kaktus

кактус

/ kʌktʊs /

---

carnation

karanfil

каранфил

/ kʌrʌnfɪl /

---

cedar

kedar

кедар

/ kedʌr /

---

cherry tree

trešnja

трешња

/ treʃnjʌ /

---

chestnut

kesten

кестен

/ kesten /

---

corn

kukuruz

кукуруз

/ kʊkʊrʊz /

---

cypress

čempres

чемпрес

/ tʃempres /

---

deciduous

listopadan

листопадан

/ lɪstɒpʌdʌn /

---

dogwood

sviba

свиба

/ svɪbʌ /

---

eucalyptus

eukaliptus

еукалиптус

/ eʊkʌlɪptus /

---

evergreen

zimzeleno

зимзелено

/ zɪmzelenɒ /

---

fern

paprat

папрат

/ pʌprʌt /

---

fertilizer

đubrivo

ђубриво

/ **dj**ʊbrɪvɒ /

fir

jela

јела

/ **je**lʌ /

flower

cvet

цвет

/ tsv**e**t /

foliage

lišće

лишће

/ **lɪ**ʃtje /

forest

šuma

шума

/ ʃʊmʌ /

fruit

voće

воће

/ **v**ɒtje /

garden
bašta
башта
/ bʌʃtʌ /

ginko
ginko
гинко
/ gɪnkɒ /

grain
zrno
зрно
/ zrnɒ /

grass
trava
трава
/ trʌvʌ /

hay
seno
сено
/ senɒ /

herb
biljka
биљка
/ bɪljkʌ /

hickory

hikori

хикори

/ hɪkɒrɪ /

ivy

bršljan

бршљан

/ brʃljʌn /

juniper

kleka

клека

/ klekʌ /

kudzu

kudzu

кудзу

/ kʊdzʊ /

leaf/leaves

list/lišće

лист/лишће

/ lɪst/lɪʃtje /

lettuce

zelena salata

зелена салата

/ zelenʌ sʌlʌtʌ /

lily

ljiljan

љиљан

/ ljɪljʌn /

magnolia

magnolija

магнолија

/ mʌgnɒlijʌ /

maple tree

javor

јавор

/ jʌvɒr /

moss

mahovina

маховина

/ mʌhɒvɪnʌ /

nut

orah

орах

/ ɒrʌh /

oak

hrast

храст

/ hrʌst /

palm tree

palma

палма

/ pʌlmʌ /

---

pine cone

šišarka

шишарка

/ ʃɪʃʌrkʌ /

---

pine tree

bor

бор

/ bɒr /

---

plant

biljka

биљка

/ bɪljkʌ /

---

peach tree

breskva

бресква

/ breskvʌ /

---

pear tree

kruška

крушка

/ krʊʃkʌ /

---

petal

latica

латица

/ lʌtɪtsʌ /

---

poison ivy

otrovni bršljen

отровни бршљен

/ ɒtrɒvnɪ brʃljen /

---

pollen

polen

polen

/ pɒlen /

---

pumpkin

tikva

tikva

/ tɪkvʌ /

---

root

koren

koren

/ kɒren /

---

roses

ruže

ruže

/ rʊʒe /

sage
žalfija
žalfija
/ ʒʌlfɪjʌ /

sap
biljni sok
biljni sok
/ **bɪ**ljni sɒk /

seed
seme
seme
/ **se**me /

shrub
žbun
žbun
/ ʒbʊn /

squash
bundeva
bundeva
/ **bʊ**ndevʌ /

soil
zemljište
zemljište
/ **ze**mljɪʃte /

stem

stabljika

stabljika

/ stʌbljɪkʌ /

---

thorn

trn

trn

/ trn /

---

tree

drvo

drvo

/ drvɒ /

---

trunk

stablo

stablo

/ stʌblɒ /

---

vegetable

povrće

povrće

/ pɒvrtje /

---

vine

loza

loza

/ lɒzʌ /

---

weed

korov

korov

/ **kɒ**rɒv /

Related Verbs
Srodni glagoli
Сродни глаголи

to fertilize

đubriti

ђубрити

/ **djʊ**brɪtɪ /

---

to gather

sakupljati

сакупљати

/ sʌ**kʊ**pljʌtɪ /

---

to grow

uzgajati

узгајати

/ ʊz**gʌ**jʌtɪ /

---

to harvest

žeti

жети

/ **ʒ**etɪ /

---

to pick

brati

брати

/ brʌtɪ/

---

to plant

saditi

садити

/ sʌdɪtɪ /

---

to plow

orati

орати

/ ɒrʌtɪ /

---

to rake

grabuljati

грабуљати

/ grʌbʊljʌtɪ /

---

to sow

sejati

сејати

/ sejʌtɪ /

---

to spray

prskati

прскати

/ prskʌtɪ /

---

to water

zalivati

заливати

/ zʌlivʌtɪ /

---

to weed

pleviti

плевити

/ **ple**vɪtɪ /

TEXT – English original Orginalni Tekst na engleskom jeziku

Farmer Smith was a kind old man. He ran the local farm and orchard. One day, while out harvesting **corn**, a bird hobbled over and sat down beside him. Farmer Smith noticed the poor little bird had a broken wing, so he gathered up his supplies and cradled the bird in one of his baskets. The bird could not fly and was helpless, so Farmer Smith decided to nurse the bird back to good health. He used a small piece of **bark** to bandage the broken wing. Every day Farmer Smith would take the bird for a walk and they would rest against the **trunk** of an old **oak tree** at the edge of the property. The farmer loved to tell the bird all about the different **plants** on his farm. He told of the **pine trees** that lined his property. These **trees** were perfect Christmas **trees**. He told of the **flowers** that grew wild near the lake, he explained how they started as a seed, and then grew into a bulb, then eventually into a beautiful **flower**. They were so colorful and vibrant; they remind the farmer of his wife. He would bring her **roses** every day for her to use on the dinner table. His wife was a wonderful cook, she could cook anything that the farmer grew; **squash, pumpkin, pears, apples, cabbage,** and many more. The way she used the **herbs** was like magic! The little bird loved to hear the stories about the farmer's wife, just hearing about her brought the bird comfort. One day, while the farmer was out **tilling** the **soil,** he heard a small sound approaching him; he turned around to see it was the little bird he had been caring for. She had learned to fly again! The farmer decided it was time for the bird to go live in the **forest** again. She was strong enough and prepared to survive on her own. It was a sad day, but the farmer took the bird into the **deciduous forest** and released her. One day, in early spring the farmer noticed a bird on his window sill. He couldn't believe his eyes, it was the same bird. He was so pleased to see the bird again, for it reminded him of his wife. Now, every spring, the bird comes to visit the farmer. He and the bird go to that old **oak tree** and Farmer Smith tells a new story about his wife. I don't know whatever happened to that bird, but it visited the farmer every year until the farmer passed away. It even visited his window sill at the hospital the year before he died. No one has ever seen it happen, but I know that the bird brings a single **rose** to Farmer Brown's resting site. Some may see the bird as a small, helpless creature, but for Farmer Smith, the bird helped to fill a void for his remaining years.

TEXT – Serbian Latin Alphabet TEKST- Srpski jezik, latinično pismo

Farmer Smit je bio dobar stari čovek. On je imao lokalnu farmu i voćnjak. Jednog dana, dok je žeo **kukuruz**, doteturala se ptica i sela pored njega. Farmer Smit je primetio da je jadnoj ptici polomljeno krilo, pa je pokupio svoje zalihe i stavio pticu u jednu od svojih korpi. Ptica nije mogla da leti i bila je bespomoćna, pa je on odlučio da je neguje dok ne ozdravi. Koristio je malo parče **kore** kako bi zavio polomljeno krilo. On je svakog dana vodio pticu u šetnju, a odmarali bi uz **stablo** starog **hrasta** na ivici njegovog imanja. Farmer je voleo da priča ptici sve o različitim **biljkama** na njegovoj farmi. Pričao je o **borovima** koji su oivičavali njegovo imanje. Ovo su bila savršena božićna **drva**. On je govorio o divljim **cvetovima** koji su rasli blizu jezera, govorio je o tome kako su počeli kao seme, a potom izrasli u pupoljke, a potom u prelepe **cvetove**. Bili su tako šareni i živopisni; podsećali su farmera na njegovu ženu. On joj je donosio **ruže** svaki dan da ih ona stavi na trpezarijski sto. Njegova žena je bila odlična kuvarica, pripremala je sve što je farmer uzgajao; **сквош, бундеве, крушке, јабуке, купус**, i mnogo još. Način na koji je koristila **bilje** je bio magičan! Mala ptica je volela da sluša priče o farmerovoj ženi, samo slušanje o njoj joj je pružalo utehu. Jednog dana dok je farmer **obrađivao zemlju**, čuo je mali zvuk kako mu se približava; okrenuo se i video da je to bila mala ptica o kojoj se brinuo. Ponovo je naučila da leti! Farmer je odlučio da je vreme za nju da ponovo živi u **šumi**. Bila je dovoljno jaka i pripremljena da preživi sama. Bio je to tužan dan, ali farmer je odneo pticu u **zimzelenu šumu** i oslobodio je. Jednog dana, u rano proleće, farmer je primetio pticu na svom prozorskom oknu. Nije mogao da veruje svojim očima, to je bila ista ptica. Bilo mu je drago što je ponovo vidi, jer ga je podsetila na njegovu suprugu. Sada, svakog proleća, ptica posećuje farmera. On i ptica odlaze do **hrasta** i farmer Smit priča novu priču o svojoj ženi. Ne znam šta se desilo toj ptici, ali je posećivala farmera svake godine sve dok on nije umro. Čak je posećivala i prozorsko okno bolnice godinu pre nego što je umro. Niko pre toga nije video ništa slično, ali znam da ptica donosi po jednu **ružu** na grob farmera Brauna. Neki mogu videti pticu kao malo, bespomoćno stvorenje, ali za farmera Smita, ptica mu je pomogla da popuni prazninu u godinama koje su mu ostale.

TEXT – Serbian Cyrilic Alphabet TEKST- Srpski jezik, ćirilićno pismo

Фармер Смит је био добар стари човек. Он је имао локалну фарму и воћњак. Једног дана, док је жео **кукуруз**, дотетурала се птица и села поред њега. Фармер Смит је приметио да је јадној птици поломљено крило, па је покупио своје залихе и ставио птицу у једну од својих корпи. Птица није могла да лети и била је беспомоћна, па је он одлучио да је негује док не оздрави. Користио је мало парче **коре** како би завио поломљено крило. Он је сваког дана водио птицу у шетњу, а одмарали би уз **стабло** старог **храста** на ивици његовог имања. Фармер је волео да прича птици све о различитим **биљкама** на његовој фарми. Причао је о **боровима** који су оивичавали његово имање. Ово су била савршена божићна **дрва**. Он је говорио о дивљим **цветовима** који су расли близу језера, говорио је о томе како су почели као семе, а потом израсли у пупољке, а потом у прелепе **цветове**. Били су тако шарени и живописни; подсећали су фармера на његову жену. Он јој је доносио **руже** сваки дан да их она стави на трпезаријски сто. Његова жена је била одлична куварица, припремала је све што је фармер узгајао; **сквош**, **бундеве**, **крушке**, **јабуке**, **купус**, и много још. Начин на који је користила **биље** је био магичан! Мала птица је волела да слуша приче о фармеровој жени, само слушање о њој јој је пружало утеху. Једног дана док је фармер **обрађивао земљу**, чуо је мали звук како му се приближава; окренуо се и видео да је то била мала птица о којој се бринуо. Поново је научила да лети! Фармер је одлучио да је време за њу да поново живи у **шуми**. Била је довољно јака и припремљена да преживи сама. Био је то тужан дан, али фармер је однео птицу у **зимзелену шуму** и ослободио је. Једног дана, у рано пролеће, фармер је приметио птицу на свом прозорском окну. Није могао да верује својим очима, то је била иста птица. Било му је драго што је поново види, јер га је подсетила на његову супругу. Сада, сваког пролећа, птица посећује фармера. Он и птица одлазе до **храста** и фармер Смит прича нову причу о својој жени. Не знам шта се десило тој птици, али је посећивала фармера сваке године све док он није умро. Чак је посећивала и прозорско окно болнице годину пре него што је умро. Нико пре тога није видео ништа слично, али знам да птица доноси по једну **ружу** на гроб фармера Брауна. Неки могу видети птицу као мало, беспомоћно створење, али за фармера Смита, птица му је помогла да попуни празнину у годинама које су му остале.

7) **Meeting Each Other**
Upoznavanja jedni drugih
Упознавање једни других

Greetings/Introductions
Pozdravi/Upoznavanja
Поздрави/Упознавања

First Line - Vocabulary Item

Second Line - Serbian Latin

Third Line - Serbian Cyrillic

Fourth Line - Serbian Pronunciation

Good morning

Dobro jutro

Добро јутро

/ dɒbrɒ jʊtrɒ /

Good afternoon

Dobar dan

Добар дан

/ dɒbʌr dʌn /

Good evening

Dobro veče

Добро вече

/ dɒbrɒ vetʃe /

Good night

Laku noć

Лаку ноћ

/ lʌkʊ nɒtj /

Hi

Zdravo

Здраво

/ zdrʌvɒ /

Hello

Zdravo

Здраво

/ zdrʌvɒ /

Have you met (name)?

Da li ste upoznali (ime)?

Да ли сте упознали (име)?

/ dʌ lɪ ste ʊpɒznʌlɪ (ime)/

Haven't we met?

Zar se nismo već upoznali?

Зар се нисмо већ упознали?

/ zʌr se nɪsmɒ vetj ʊpɒznʌlɪ /

How are you?

Kako si?

Како си?

/ kʌkɒ sɪ /

How are you today?

Kako si danas?

Како си данас?

/ kʌkɒ sɪ dʌnʌs /

How do you do?

Drago mi je

Драго ми је

/ drʌgɒ mɪ je /

How's it going?

Kako ste?

Како сте?

/ kʌkɒ ste /

I am (name)

Ja sam (ime)

Ја сам (име)

/ jʌ sʌm (ɪme)/

I don't think we've met.

Mislim da se nismo upoznali

Мислим да се нисмо упознали

/ mɪslɪm dʌ se nɪsmɒ ʊpɒznʌlɪ /

It's nice to meet you.

Drago mi je da sam te upoznao

Драго ми је да сам те упознао

/ drʌgɒ mɪ je dʌ sʌm te ʊpɒznʌɒ /

Meet (name)

Upoznajte (ime)

Упознајте (име)

/ ʊpɒznʌjte (**ɪme**)/

My friends call me (nickname)

Moji prijatelji me zovu (nadimak)

Моји пријатељи ме зову (надимак)

/ **mɒ**jɪ **prɪ**jʌteljɪ me **zɒ**vu (nʌdɪmʌk)/

My name is (name)

Moje ime je (ime)

Моје име је (име)

/ **mɒ**je ɪme je (**ɪme**) /

Nice to meet you

Drago mi je

Драго ми је

/ **drʌ**gɒ mɪ je /

Nice to see you again.

Drago mi je da te ponovo vidim

Драго ми је да те поново видим

/ **drʌ**gɒ mɪ je dʌ te **pɒ**nɒvɒ **vɪ**dɪm /

Pleased to meet you.

Drago mi je

Драго ми је

/ **drʌ**gɒ mɪ je /

This is (name)

Ovo je (ime)

Ово је (име)

/ ɒvɒ je (ɪme) /

What's your name?

Kako se zoveš?

Како се зовеш?

/ kʌkɒ se zɒveʃ /

Who are you?

Ko ste Vi?

Ко сте Ви?

/ kɒ ste vɪ /

Greeting Answers

Odgovori na pozdrav

Одговори на поздрав

Fine, thanks

Dobro, hvala

Добро, хвала

/ dɒbrɒ hvʌlʌ /

I'm exhausted

Iscrpljen sam

Исцрпљен сам

/ ɪscrpljen sʌm /

I'm okay

Dobro sam

Добро сам

/ dɒbrɒ sʌm /

I'm sick

Nije mi dobro

Није ми добро

/ nɪje mɪ dɒbrɒ /

I'm tired

Umoran sam

Уморан сам

/ ʊmɒrʌn sʌm /

Not too bad

Nisam loše

Нисам лоше

/ nɪsʌm lɒʃe /

Not too well, actually

Nisam baš dobro, zapravo

Нисам баш добро, заправо

/ nɪsʌm bʌʃ dɒbrɒ zʌprʌvɒ /

Very well

Vrlo dobro

Врло добро

/ vrlɒ dɒbrɒ /

Saying Goodbye
Pozdraviti se
Поздравити се

Bye

Doviđenja

Довиђења

/ dɒvɪ**dje**njʌ /

Good bye

Doviđenja

Довиђења

/ dɒvɪ**dje**njʌ /

Good night

Laku noć

Лаку ноћ

/ **lʌ**kʊ nɒć /

See you

Vidimo se

Видимо се

/ **vɪ**dɪmɒ se /

See you later

Vidimo se kasnije

Видимо се касније

/ **vɪ**dɪmɒ se **kʌ**snɪje /

See you next week

Vidimo se sledeće nedelje

Видимо се следеће недеље

/ **vɪ**dɪmɒ se **sle**detje **ne**delje /

See you soon

Vidimo se uskoro

Видимо се ускоро

/ **vɪ**dɪmɒ se ʊskɒrɒ /

See you tomorrow

Vidimo se sutra

Видимо се сутра

/ **vɪ**dɪmɒ se sʊtrʌ /

Courtesy
Uljudnost
Уљудност

Excuse me

Izvinite

Извините

/ ɪz**vɪ**nɪte /

Pardon me

Izvinite

Извините

/ ɪz**vɪ**nɪte /

I'm sorry

Žao mi je

Жао ми је

/ ʒɑɒ mɪ je /

Thanks

Hvala

Хвала

/ hvʌlʌ /

Thank you

Hvala Vam

Хвала Вам

/ hvʌlʌ vʌm /

You're welcome

Nema na čemu

Нема на чему

/ nemʌ nʌ tʃemu /

Special Greetings
Posebni pozdravi
Посебни поздрави

Congratulations

Čestitke

Честитке

/ tʃestɪtke /

Get well soon

Brzo se oporavi

Брзо се опорави

/ **br**zɒ se ɒpɒrʌvɪ /

Good luck

Srećno

Срећно

/ **sre**tjno /

Happy New Year

Srećna Nova godina

Срећна Нова година

/ **sre**tjnʌ nɒvʌ gɒdɪnʌ /

Happy Easter

Srećan Uskrs

Срећан Ускрс

/ **sre**tjʌn ʊskrs /

Merry Christmas

Srećan Božić

Срећан Божић

/ **sre**tjʌn **bo**ʒɪtj /

Well done

Vrlo dobro

Врло добро

/ **vr**lɒ **dɒ**brɒ /

Related Verbs
Srodni glagoli
Сродни глаголи

to greet

pozdraviti

поздравити

/ pɒzdrʌvɪtɪ /

---

to meet

sresti

срести

/ **sre**stɪ /

---

to say

reći

рећи

/ **re**tjɪ /

---

to shake hands

rukovati se

руковати се

/ **rʊ**kɒvʌtɪ se /

---

to talk

pričati

причати

/ **prɪ**tʃʌtɪ /

---

to thank

zahvaliti

захвалити

/ zʌhvʌlɪtɪ /

TEXT – English original Orginalni Tekst na engleskom jeziku

This is the story of a man named Pop. He just started a new job as a greeter at the local discount store. His son was so proud, he gave him a card that said, **"Congratulations"**. He is a little nervous because he has never been a store greeter before. Throughout the day, there are so many customers going in and out of the store, sometimes Pop forgets what he should say. **"Pleased to meet you"** or **"Can I help you out?"** are good options for being polite. His manager assured him, saying, "You will be just fine, so don't worry." He begins the work day with a smile on his face, but by the end of the day, his smile is erased. **"Good morning,"** he says with a smile to the nice lady walking down the produce aisle. **"How are you doing?"** asked Pop, but she must not have heard him, because she didn't stop to say **hello**. "Hmm", said Pop, I guess she didn't hear me because a polite person would have said something like, **'Fine, how are you?'** or **'I'm fine, thank you.'** Next there was man with a bushy white beard, he looked very friendly and kind. Pop greeted him politely and said, **"Happy New Year!"** The man just grunted and went on his way, I guess he wasn't friendly after all. Pop replied, **"Have a good day!"** The next several customers were polite and spoke to him. Some of the customers said, **"How do you do?"** and one said, **"My name is Jim. What is your name?"** As the day went on, Pop got really tired and his **greetings** were losing not seeming as effective as earlier in the day. His manager was upset, but gave him another chance. He warned Pop that just saying **"Hi"** or **"Hello"** wasn't enough for the friendly environment our customers are used to. "If you want to make a good impression, you have to be polite. You can say something like, **'Merry Christmas'** or **'Good day to you, sir'**, but please be nice to everyone you meet. Finally, as the end of the day was nearing, Pop was very happy to finally be able to say, "**Good night**." He went home without his smile, but said tomorrow is a new day and I will make sure to smile for everyone.

TEXT –Serbian Latin Alphabet TEKST- Srpski jezik, latinično pismo

Ovo je priča o čoveku po imenu Pop. On je upravo počeo da radi na novom poslu kao pozdravljač u lokalnom diskontu. Njegov sin je bio veoma ponosan, dao mu je karticu sa natpisom "Čestitam." On je malo nervozan jer nikada pre nije radio taj posao. Tokom dana, ima mnogo mušterija koje ulaze i izlaze iz radnje, ponekad Pop zaboravi šta treba da kaže. "Drago mi je da Vas vidim" ili "**Da li mogu da Vam pomognem**?" su dobre opcije kako biti uljudan. Njegov menadžer ga je ohrabrio tako što mu je rekao "Bićeš dobar, zato ne brini." On počinje radni dan sa osmehom na licu, ali do kraja dana njegov osmeh je obrisan. "**Dobro jutro**" kaže sa osmehom lepoj dami koja prolazi između rafova. "**Kako ste**?" pitao je Pop, ali mora da ga ona nije čula jer nije stala da mu kaže **zdravo**. "Hmm" rekao je Pop, pretpostavljam da me nije čula jer bi vaspitana osoba rekla nešto poput "**Dobro, kako ste Vi**?" ili "**Dobro sam, hvala**." Zatim je bio čovek sa gustombelom bradom, izgledao je prijateljski i kulturno. Pop ga je kulturno pozdravio i rekao mu "**Srećna Nova godina!**" čovek je samo promrmljao i nastavio, pretpostavljam da ipak nije prijateljski raspoložen. Pop je odgovorio, "**Prijatan dan!**" nekoliko narednih mušterija je bilo kulturno i razgovaralo s njim. Neke od mušterija su rekle "**Kako ste**" a jedna je rekla "**Moje ime je Džim. Kako se ti zoveš**?" kako je dan prolazio, Pop se umorio a činilo se da njegovi **pozdravi** više nisu toliko efikasni kao na početku dana. Njegov menadžer je bio nervozan, ali mu je dao još jednu priliku. Rekao je Popu da "**Ćao** " i "**Zdravo**" jednostavno nisu dovoljni za prijateljsko okruženje na koje su njihove mušterije navikle. "Ako želiš da ostaviš dobar utisak, moraš biti uljudan. Možeš da kažeš nešto tipa **Srećan Božić** ili **Lepo Vas je videti danas**, gospodine, ali molim te da budeš prijatan prema svakome koga sretneš. " Na kraju, kako se približava kraj dana, Pop je bio veoma srećan da konačno kaže "**Laku noć**." Otišao je kući bez svog osmeha, ali je rekao da je sutra novi dan i da će se pobrinuti da se smeši svima.

TEXT –Serbian Cyrilic Alphabet TEKST- Srpski jezik, ćirilićno pismo

Ово је прича о човеку по имену Поп. Он је управо почео да ради на новом послу као поздрављач у локалном дисконту. Његов син је био веома поносан, дао му је картицу са натписом "**Честитам**." Он је мало нервозан јер никада пре није радио тај посао. Током дана, има много муштерија које улазе и излазе из радње, понекад Поп заборави шта треба да каже. "**Драго ми је да Вас видим**" или "**Да ли могу да Вам помогнем**?" су добре опције како бити уљудан. Његов менаџер га је охрабрио тако што му је рекао "Бићеш добар, зато не брини." Он почиње радни дан са осмехом на лицу, али до краја дана његов осмех је обрисан. "**Добро јутро**" каже са осмехом лепој дами која пролази између рафова. "**Како сте**?" питао је Поп, али мора да га она није чула јер није стала да му каже **здраво**. "Хмм" рекао је Поп, претпостављам да ме није чула јер би васпитана особа рекла нешто типа "**Добро, како сте Ви**?" или "**Добро сам, хвала**." Затим је био човек са густомбелом брадом, изгледао је пријатељски и културно. Поп га је културно поздравио и рекао му "**Срећна Нова година**!" човек је само промрмљао и наставио, претпостављам да ипак није пријатељски расположен. Поп је одговорио, "**Пријатан дан**!" неколико наредних муштерија је било културно и разговарало с њим. Неке од муштерија су рекле "**Како сте**" а једна је рекла "**Моје име је Џим. Како се ти зовеш**?" како је дан пролазио, Поп се уморио а чинило се да његови **поздрави** више нису толико ефикасни као на почетку дана. Његов менаџер је био нервозан, али му је дао још једну прилику. Рекао је Попу да "**Ћао**" и "**Здраво**" једноставно нису довољни за пријатељско окружење на које су њихове муштерије навикле. "Ако желиш да оставиш добар утисак, мораш бити уљудан. Можеш да кажеш нешто типа **Срећан Божић** или **Лепо**

Вас је видети данас, господине, али молим те да будеш пријатан према свакоме кога сретнеш. ” На крају, како се приближава крај дана, Поп је био веома срећан да коначно каже "**Лаку ноћ**." Отишао је кући без свог осмеха, али је рекао да је сутра нови дан и да ће се побринути да се смеши свима.

8) House
Kuća
Кућа

First Line - Vocabulary Item
Second Line - Serbian Latin
Third Line - Serbian Cyrillic
Fourth Line - Serbian Pronunciation

air conditioner
klima
клима
/ **klɪ**mʌ /

appliances
aparati
апарати
/ ʌpʌrʌtɪ /

attic
potkrovlje
поткровље
/ **pɒ**tkrɒvlje /

awning
nadstrešnica
надстрешница
/ **nʌ**dstreʃnɪtsʌ /

backyard

dvorište

двориште

/ **dvɒ**rɪʃte /

balcony

balkon

балкон

/ **bʌ**lkɒn /

basement

podrum

подрум

/ **pɒ**drʊm /

bathroom

kupatilo

купатило

/ kʊ**pʌ**tɪlɒ /

bath tub

kada

када

/ **kʌ**dʌ /

bed

krevet

кревет

/ **kre**vet /

bedroom

spavaća soba

спаваћа соба

/ spʌvʌtjʌ sɒbʌ /

blanket

ćebe

ћебе

/ tjebe /

blender

blender

блендер

/ blender /

blinds

roletne

ролетне

/ rɒletne /

bookshelf/bookcase

polica za knjige

полица за књиге

/ pɒlɪtsʌ za knjɪge /

bowl

činija

чинија

/ tʃɪnɪjʌ /

cabinet

ormar

ормар

/ ɒrmʌr /

---

carpet

tepih

тепих

/ **te**pɪh /

---

carport

nadstrešnica za kola

надстрешница за кола

/ **n**ʌdstreʃnɪtsʌ zʌ **k**ɒlʌ /

---

ceiling

plafon

плафон

/ **pl**ʌfɒn /

---

cellar

podrum

подрум

/ **p**ɒdrʊm /

---

chair

stolica

столица

/ **st**ɒlɪtsʌ /

chimney

dimnjak

димњак

/ **dɪ**mnjʌk /

clock

zidni sat

зидни сат

/ **zɪ**dnɪ sʌt /

closet

plakar

плакар

/ **plʌ**kʌr /

computer

kompjuter

компјутер

/ **kɒ**mp**jʊ**ter /

couch

kauč

кауч

/ **kʌ**ʊtʃ /

counter

šank

шанк

/ **ʃʌ**nk /

crib

krevetac

креветац

/ krevetʌts /

cupboard

kredenac

креденац

/ **kre**denʌts /

cup

šolja

шоља

/ ʃɒljʌ /

curtain

zavesa

завеса

/ zʌvesʌ /

desk

sto

сто

/ stɒ /

dining room

trpezarija

трпезарија

/ trpezʌrɪjʌ /

dishes

posuđe

посуђе

/ **pɒ**sʊdje /

---

dishwasher

mašina za sudove

машина за судове

/ mʌʃınʌ zʌ **sʊ**dɒve /

---

door

vrata

врата

/ **vrʌ**tʌ /

---

doorbell

zvono

звоно

/ **zvɒ**nɒ /

---

doorknob

kvaka

квака

/ **kvʌ**kʌ /

---

doorway

ulaz

улаз

/ **ʊ**lʌz /

drapes

draperje

драперје

/ **drʌ**perje /

---

drawer

fioka

фиока

/ fɪɒkʌ /

---

driveway

prilaz

прилаз

/ **prɪ**lʌz /

---

dryer

sušilica

сушилица

/ **sʊ**ʃɪlɪtsʌ /

---

duct

cev

цев

/ ts**e**v /

---

exterior

eksterijer

екстеријер

/ ekste**rɪ**jer /

---

family room

dnevna soba

дневна соба

/ dnevnʌ sɒbʌ /

fan

ventilator

вентилатор

/ ventɪlʌtɒr /

faucet

slavina

славина

/ slʌvɪnʌ /

fence

ograda

ограда

/ ɒgrʌdʌ /

fireplace

kamin

камин

/ kʌmɪn /

floor

pod

под

/ pɒd /

foundation

temelj

темељ

/ **te**melj /

---

frame

okvir

оквир

/ **ɒ**kvɪr /

---

freezer

zamrzivač

замрзивач

/ zʌm**rzɪ**vʌtʃ /

---

furnace

peć

пећ

/ p**e**tj /

---

furniture

nameštaj

намештај

/ **nʌ**meʃtʌj /

---

garage

garaža

гаража

/ gʌ**rʌ**ʒʌ /

---

garden

bašta

башта

/ bʌʃtʌ /

---

grill

roštilj

роштиљ

/ rɒʃtɪlj /

---

gutters

oluci

олуци

/ ɒlutsɪ /

---

hall/hallway

hodnik

ходник

/ hɒdnɪk /

---

hamper

korpa

корпа

/ kɒrpʌ /

---

heater

radijator

радијатор

/ rʌdɪjʌtɒr /

insulation

izolacija

изолација

/ ɪzɒlʌtsɪjʌ /

jacuzzi tub

đakuzi

ђакузи

/ djʌkʊzɪ /

key

ključ

кључ

/ kljʊtʃ /

kitchen

kuhinja

кухиња

/ kʊhɪnjʌ /

ladder

merdevine

мердевине

/ merdevɪne /

lamp

lampa

лампа

/ lʌmpʌ /

landing

hodnik

ходник

/ **hɒ**dnɪk /

laundry

vešernica

вешерница

/ veʃernɪtsʌ /

lawn

travnjak

травњак

/ **trʌ**vnjʌk /

lawnmower

kosilica

косилица

/ **kɒ**sɪlɪtsʌ /

library

biblioteka

библиотека

/ bɪblɪɒ**tek**ʌ /

light

svetlo

светло

/ **sve**tlɒ /

linen closet

ormar za posteljinu

ормар за постељину

/ ɒrmʌr za pɒsteljɪnʊ /

living room

dnevna soba

дневна соба

/ dnevnʌ sɒbʌ /

lock

brava

брава

/ brʌvʌ /

loft

potkrovlje

поткровље

/ pɒtkrɒvlje /

mailbox

poštansko sanduče

поштанско сандуче

/ pɒʃtʌnskɒ sʌndutʃe /

mantle

ogrtač

огртач

/ ɒgrtʌtʃ /

master bedroom

glavna spavaća soba

главна спаваћа соба

/ glʌvnʌ spʌvʌtjʌ sɒbʌ /

microwave

mikrotalasna

микроталасна

/ mɪkrɒtʌlʌsnʌ /

mirror

ogledalo

огледало

/ ɒgledʌlɒ /

neighborhood

komšiluk

комшилук

/ kɒmʃɪlʊk /

nightstand

stočić

сточић

/ stɒtʃɪtj /

office

kancelarija

канцеларија

/ kʌntselʌrɪjʌ /

oven

rerna

рерна

/ rernʌ/

---

painting

slika

слика

/ slɪkʌ /

---

paneling

oblaganje

облагање

/ oblʌgʌnje /

---

pantry

ostava

остава

/ ɒstʌvʌ /

---

patio

unutrašnje dvorište

унутрашње двориште

/ ʊnʊtrʌʃnje dvɒrɪʃte /

---

picnic table

sto za piknik

сто за пикник

/ stɒ za pɪknɪk /

picture

fotografija

фотографија

/ fɒtɒgrʌfijʌ /

picture frame

okvir za sliku

оквир за слику

/ ɒkvɪr za slɪkʊ /

pillow

jastuk

јастук

/ jʌstʊk /

plates

tanjiri

тањири

/ tʌnjɪrɪ /

plumbing

vodovodne instalacije

водоводне инсталације

/ vɒdɒvɒdne ɪnstʌlʌtsɪje /

pool

bazen

базен

/ bʌzen /

porch

trem

трем

/ trɛm /

---

queen bed

francuski ležaj

француски лежај

/ frʌncʊskɪ leʒʌj /

---

quilt

jorgan

јорган

/ jɒrgʌn /

---

railing

ograda

ограда

/ ɒgrʌdʌ /

---

range

domet

домет

/ dɒmet /

---

refrigerator

frižider

фрижидер

/ frɪʒɪder /

---

remote control

daljinski

даљински

/ dʌljɪnskɪ /

---

roof

krov

кров

/ krɒv /

---

room

soba

соба

/ sɒbʌ /

---

rug

tepih

тепих

/ tepɪh /

---

screen door

vetrobranska vrata

ветробранска врата

/ vetrɒbrʌnskʌ vrʌtʌ /

---

shed

šupa

шупа

/ ʃʊpʌ /

shelf/shelves

polica/police

полица/полице

/ pɒlɪtsʌ/pɒlɪtse /

---

shingle

tegola

тегола

/ tegɒlʌ /

---

shower

tuš

туш

/ tʊʃ /

---

shutters

kapci

капци

/ kʌptsɪ /

---

siding

pokrivanje zidova

покривање зидова

/ pɒkrɪvʌnje zɪdɒvʌ /

---

sink

sudopera

судопера

/ sʊdɒperʌ /

---

sofa

sofa

софа

/ sɒfʌ /

stairs/staircase

stepenice

степенице

/ stepenɪtse /

step

stepenik

степеник

/ stepenɪk /

stoop

stepenište

степениште

/ stepenɪʃte /

stove

šporet

шпорет

/ ʃpɒret /

study

radna soba

радна соба

/ rʌdnʌ sɒbʌ /

table

sto

сто

/ stɒ /

---

telephone

telefon

телефон

/ telefɒn /

---

television

televizor

телевизор

/ televɪzɒr /

---

toaster

toster

тостер

/ tɒster /

---

toilet

toalet

тоалет

/ toʌlet /

---

towel

peškir

пешкир

/ peʃkɪr /

---

trash can

kanta

kanta

/ kʌntʌ /

---

trim

oprema

oprema

/ ɒpremʌ /

---

upstairs

gornji sprat

gornji sprat

/ gɒrnjɪ sprʌt /

---

utility room

ostava

ostava

/ ɒstʌvʌ /

---

vacuum

usisavati

usisavati

/ ʊsɪsʌvʌtɪ /

---

vanity

stočić sa ogledalcem

stočić sa ogledalcem

/ stɒtʃɪtj sʌ ɒgledʌltsem /

---

vase

vaza

vaza

/ vʌzʌ /

vent

ventilacija

ventilacija

/ ventɪlʌtsɪjʌ /

wall

zid

zid

/ zɪd /

wardrobe

garderober

garderober

/ gʌrderɒber /

washer/washing

mašina za pranje/pranje

mašina za pranje/pranje

/ maʃɪnʌ zʌ **prʌ**nje/**prʌ**nje /

machine

mašina

mašina

/ mʌʃɪnʌ /

waste basket

korpa

korpa

/ **kɒ**rpʌ /

water heater

bojler

bojler

/ **bɒ**jler /

welcome mat

otirač

otirač

/ ɒtɪrʌtʃ /

window

prozor

prozor

/ **prɒ**zɒr /

window pane

prozorsko okno

prozorsko okno

/ **prɒ**zɒrskɒ ɒknɒ /

window sill

prozorski prag

prozorski prag

/ **prɒ**zɒrskɪ prʌg /

yard

dvorište

dvorište

/ **dvɒ**rɪʃte /

Related Verbs

Srodni glagoli

Сродни глаголи

---

to build

sagraditi

саградити

/ sʌgrʌdɪtɪ /

---

to buy

kupiti

купити

/ **kʊ**pɪtɪ /

---

to clean

očistiti

очистити

/ ɒtʃɪstɪtɪ /

---

to decorate

ukrasiti

украсити

/ ʊkrʌsɪtɪ /

---

to leave

napustiti

напустити

/ nʌpʊstɪtɪ /

to move in

useliti se

уселити се

/ ʊselɪtɪ se /

to move out

iseliti se

иселити се

/ ɪselɪtɪ se /

to renovate

renovirati

реновирати

/ renɒvɪrʌtɪ /

to repair

popraviti

поправити

/ pɒprʌvɪtɪ /

to sell

prodati

продати

/ prodʌtɪ /

to show

pokazati

показати

/ pɒkʌzʌtɪ /

---

to view

pogledati

погледати

/ pɒgledʌtɪ /

---

to visit

posetiti

посетити

/ pɒsetɪtɪ /

---

to work

raditi

радити

/ rʌdɪtɪ /

TEXT – Enlish original Orginalni Tekst na engleskom jeziku

Mike and Linda just bought their first **house**. It is a not a large house, but it is very cozy. It is in a very nice **neighborhood** and has a cute, well-manicured **lawn**. It has a small front **porch**, which will be nice to relax on in the evenings after work. The **exterior** is light blue with a dark blue **door** and **shutters**. It has a nice size **garage** that is big enough for both of their cars and a small **shed** out back for their **lawnmower**. The **backyard** is small, but has a cute little swing set. One day, maybe they will have kids to enjoy it. The **living room** is very spacious and is beautifully decorated in greens and blues. The **walls** are painted light blue and the **curtains** are patterned green and blue. The **couch** and **chair** are very comfortable and roomy enough for the few guests they may have on occasion. Mike is very excited about the new **television** they had installed on the **wall** above the **fireplace**. The **kitchen** is small, yet functional. It has a **refrigerator**, a **dishwasher**, an **oven**, and a built-in **microwave**. There is not much storage, so Linda will have to be very organized. The **walls** are painted yellow and it has a nice floral border. Linda did not pick it out, but it suits her taste well. The **house** has three **bedrooms**, which gives their family room to grow. The **master bedroom** is big enough to fit their **queen bed**, two **nightstands**, and a **dresser**. Linda has already picked out **curtains** to match the bedding. The **walls** are painted beige, but Linda thinks she can brighten the **room** with other decor. Linda's favorite part of the house is the master **bathroom**; it has a **jacuzzi tub** and she can't wait to try it out. It also has a separate **shower** and a double **vanity**. Mike works from home, so he plans to use one of the other, even smaller **bedrooms** as a home **office**. There is not a lot of space, but enough for his **desk**, **computer**, and a **bookshelf**. The back **porch** is nice and has a charcoal **grill** and a **picnic table**. Mike loves to cook on the **grill**, so it will be put to good use. They will need to get a **washing machine** and **dryer** for the **laundry room**, it is small, but it has a **sink**, which is very helpful when washing clothes. Overall, Mike and Linda picked out an excellent first home. It fits their budget, as well as their taste perfectly!

TEXT – Serbian Latin Alphabet TEKST- Srpski jezik, latinično pismo

Majk i Linda su upravo kupili svoju prvu **kuću**. To je nije velika kuća, ali je veoma udobna. Ona je u vrlo lepom **naselju** i ima sladak, dobro održavani **travnjak**. Ona ima mali **trem**, koji će biti lep za opuštanje uveče posle posla. **Eksterijer** je svetlo plave boje sa teget **vratima** i **roletnama**. Ima lepu **garažu** odgovarajuće veličine koja je dovoljno velika za oba njihova automobila i malu **šupu** pozadi za njihovu **kosilicu**. **Dvorište** je malo, ali ima slatku malu **ljuljašku**. Jednog dana, možda će imati decu da uživaju u njoj. **Dnevni boravak** je veoma prostrana i lepo uređena prostorija u zelenoj i plavoj boji. **Zidovi** su ofarbani svetlo plavo a **zavese** su u dezenu zelene i plave boje. **Kauč** i **fotelja** su veoma udobni i prostrani i dovoljno za nekoliko gostiju koje mogu imati povremeno. Majk je veoma uzbuđen zbog novog **televizora** koji su instalirali na **zidu** iznad **kamina**. **Kuhinja** je mala, ali funkcionalna. Ima **frižider**, **mašinu za pranje suđa**, **rernu** i ugrađenu **mikrotalasnu**. Nema mnogo mesta za skladištenje, tako će Linda morati da bude veoma organizovana. **Zidovi** su ofarbani žuto i imaju lep cvetni rub. Linda ga nije izabrala, ali dobro odgovara njenom ukusu. **Kuća** ima tri **spavaće sobe**, što daje ovoj porodici mesta za povećanje. **Glavna spavaća soba** je dovoljno velika da stane veliki **krevet**, dva **stočića** i **komode**. Linda je već izabrala **zavese** da odgovaraju posteljini. **Zidovi** su ofarbani bež, ali Linda misli da može uljepšati sobu drugim dekorom. Lindin omiljeni deo kuće je **veliko kupatilo**; ima **đakuzi** i ona ne može čeka da ga isproba. Ona takođe ima poseban **tuš** i svoj **ormarić sa ogledalcem**. Majk radi od kuće, tako da planira da koristi jednu od drugih, čak manjih **spavaćih soba** kao **kućnu kancelariju**. Nema puno prostora, ali ima dovoljno za njegov **sto**, **kompjuter** i **policu za knjige**. Stražnja **veranda** je lepa i ima **roštilj** na ćumur i **sto za piknik**. Majk voli da kuva na **roštilju**, tako da će biti dobro iskorišćen. Oni će morati da nabaveveš **mašinu** i **sušilicu** za **perionicu**, ona je mala, ali ima **lavabo**, što je veoma korisno prilikom pranja odeće. Generalno, Majk i Linda su izabrali odličan prvi dom. Savršeno odgovara njihovom budžetu, kao i njihovom ukusu!

TEXT – Serbian Cyrilic Alphabet TEKST- Srpski jezik, ćirilično pismo

Мајк и Линда су управо купили своју прву **кућу**. То је није велика кућа, али је веома удобна. Она је у врло лепом **насељу** и има сладак, добро одржавани **травњак**. Она има мали **трем**, који ће бити леп за опуштање увече после посла. **Екстеријер** је светло плаве боје са тегет **вратима** и **ролетнама**. Има лепу **гаражу** одговарајуће величине која је довољно велика за оба њихова аутомобила и малу **шупу** позади за њихову **косилицу**.

Двориште је мало, али има слатку малу **љуљашку**. Једног дана, можда ће имати децу да уживају у њој. **Дневни боравак** је веома пространа и лепо уређена просторија у зеленој и плавој боји. **Зидови** су офарбани светло плаво а **завесе** су у дезену зелене и плаве боје. **Кауч** и **фотеља** су веома удобни и пространи и довољно за неколико гостију које могу имати повремено. Мајк је веома узбуђен због новог **телевизора** који су инсталирали на **зиду** изнад **камина**. **Кухиња** је мала, али функционална. Има **фрижидер**, **машину за прање суђа**, **рерну** и уграђену **микроталасну**. Нема много места за складиштење, тако ће Линда морати да буде веома организована. **Зидови** су офарбани жуто и имају леп цветни руб. Линда га није изабрала, али добро одговара њеном укусу. **Кућа** има три **спаваће собе**, што даје овој породици места за повећање. **Главна спаваћа соба** је довољно велика да стане **велики кревет**, два **сточића** и **комоде**. Линда је већ изабрала **завесе** да одговарају постељини. **Зидови** су офарбани беж, али Линда мисли да може уљепшати собу другим декором. Линдин омиљени део куће је велико купатило; има **ђакузи** и она не може чека да га испроба. Она такође има посебан **туш** и свој **ормарић са огледалцем**. Мајк ради од куће, тако да планира да користи једну од других, чак мањих **спаваћих соба** као **кућну канцеларију**. Нема пуно простора, али има довољно за његов **сто**, **компјутер** и **полицу за књиге**. Стражња **веранда** је лепа и има **роштиљ** на ћумур и **сто за пикник**. Мајк воли да кува на **роштиљу**, тако да ће бити добро искоришћен. Они ће морати да набаве **веш машину** и **сушилицу** за **перионицу**, она је мала, али има **лавабо**, што је веома корисно приликом прања одеће. Генерално, Мајк и Линда су изабрали одличан први дом. Савршено одговара њиховом буџету, као и њиховом укусу!

9) Arts and Entertainment
Umetnost i zabava
Уметност и забава

First Line - Vocabulary Item
Second Line - Serbian Latin
Third Line - Serbian Cyrillic
Fourth Line - Serbian Pronunciation

3-D
3-D
3-Д
/ trɪ de /

---

action movie
akcioni film
акциони филм
/ ʌktsɪɒnɪ film /

---

actor/actress
glumac/glumica
глумац/глумица
/ glʊmʌts/glʊmɪtsʌ /

---

album
album
албум
/ ʌlbʊm /

---

alternative

alternativa

алтернатива

/ ʌlternʌtɪvʌ /

amphitheater

amfiteatar

амфитеатар

/ ʌmfɪteʌtʌr /

animation

animacija

анимација

/ ʌnɪmʌtsɪjʌ /

artist

umetnik

уметник

/ ʊmetnɪk /

audience

publika

публика

/ pʊblɪkʌ /

ballerina

balerina

балерина

/ bʌlerɪnʌ /

ballet

balet

балет

/ bʌlet /

---

band

bend

бенд

/ bend /

---

blues

bluz

блуз

/ blʊz /

---

caption

naslov

наслов

/ nʌslɒv /

---

carnival

karneval

карневал

/ kʌrnevʌl /

---

cast

postava

постава

/ pɒstʌvkʌ /

---

choreographer

koreograf

кореограф

/ kɒreɒgrʌf /

cinema

bioskop

биоскоп

/ bɪɒskɒp /

classic

klasik

класик

/ klʌsɪk /

comedy

komedija

комедија

/ kɒmedɪjʌ /

commercial

komercijalan

комерцијалан

/ kɒmertsɪjʌlʌn /

composer

kompozitor

композитор

/ kɒmpɒzɪtɒr /

concert

koncert

концерт

/ **kɒ**ntsert /

conductor

dirigent

диригент

/ dɪrɪ**gen**t /

contemporary

savremen

савремен

/ **s**ʌvremen /

country

kantri

кантри

/ **k**ʌntrɪ /

credits

zasluge

заслуге

/ **z**ʌslʊge /

dancer

plesač

плесач

/ **ple**satʃ /

director

režiser

режисер

/ reʒɪser /

---

documentary

dokumentarac

документарац

/ dɒkʊmentʌrʌts /

---

drama

drama

драма

/ drʌmʌ /

---

drummer

bubnjar

бубњар

/ bʊbnjʌr /

---

duet

duet

дует

/ dʊet /

---

episode

epizoda

епизода

/ epɪzɒdʌ /

---

event

događaj

догађај

/ dɒgʌdjʌj /

exhibit

izložiti

изложити

/ ɪzlɒʒɪtɪ /

exhibition

izložba

изложба

/ ɪzlɒʒbʌ /

fair

vašar

вашар

/ vʌʃʌr /

fantasy

fantazija

фантазија

/ fʌntʌzɪjʌ /

feature/feature film

igrani film

играни филм

/ ɪgrʌnɪ fɪlm /

film

film

филм

/ fɪlm /

---

flick

zvrčka

зврчка

/ zvrtʃkʌ /

---

folk

narodni

народни

/ nʌrɒdnɪ /

---

gallery

galerija

галерија

/ gʌlerɪjʌ /

---

genre

žanr

жанр

/ ʒʌnr /

---

gig

tezga

тезга

/ tezgʌ /

---

group

grupa

група

/ **grʊ**pʌ /

guitar

gitara

гитара

/ gɪt**ʌ**rʌ /

guitarist

gitarista

гитариста

/ gɪt**ʌ**rɪstʌ /

hip-hop

hip-hop

хип-хоп

/ hɪp-hɒp /

horror

horor

хорор

/ **hɒ**rɒr /

inspirational

inspirišući

инспиришући

/ ɪns**pɪ**rɪʃʊtjɪ /

jingle

džingl

џингл

/ **dʒ**ɪngl /

---

legend

legenda

легенда

/ **le**gendʌ /

---

lyrics

tekst

текст

/ **te**kst /

---

magician

mađioničar

мађионичар

/ mʌdjɪɒnɪtʃʌr /

---

microphone

mikrofon

микрофон

/ **mɪ**krɒfɒn /

---

motion picture

film

филм

/ **fɪ**lm /

---

movie director

filmski režiser

филмски режисер

/ fɪlmskɪ reʒɪser /

---

movie script

filmski tekst

филмски текст

/ fɪlmskɪ tekst /

---

museum

muzej

музеј

/ mʊzej /

---

music

muzika

музика

/ mʊzɪkʌ /

---

musical

mjuzikl

мјузикл

/ mjʊzɪkl /

---

musician

muzičar

музичар

/ mʊzitʃʌr /

---

mystery

misterija

мистерија

/ **mɪ**sterɪjʌ /

new age

novo doba

ново доба

/ **nɒ**vɒ **d**ɒbʌ /

opera

opera

опера

/ **ɒ**perʌ /

opera house

opera

опера

/ **ɒ**perʌ /

orchestra

orkestar

оркестар

/ **ɒ**rkestʌr /

painter

slikar

сликар

/ **slɪ**kʌr /

painting

slika

слика

/ slɪkʌ /

parade

parada

парада

/ pʌrʌdʌ /

performance

izvođenje

извођење

/ ɪzvɒdjenje /

pianist

pijanista

пијаниста

/ pɪjʌnɪstʌ /

picture

slika

слика

/ slɪkʌ /

play

predstava

представа

/ predstʌvʌ /

playwright

pisac

писац

/ **pɪ**sʌts /

---

pop

pop

поп

/ p**ɒ**p /

---

popcorn

kokice

кокице

/ **kɒ**kɪtse /

---

producer

producent

продуцент

/ prɒ**dʊ**tsent /

---

rap

rep

реп

/ r**e**p /

---

reggae

rege

реге

/ **re**ge /

---

repertoire

repertoar

репертоар

/ repertɒʌr /

---

rok

rok

рок

/ rɒk /

---

role

uloga

улога

/ ʊlɒgʌ /

---

romance

romansa

романса

/ rɒmʌnsʌ /

---

scene

scena

сцена

/ stsenʌ /

---

science fiction

naučna fantastika

научна фантастика

/ nʌutʃnʌ fʌntʌstɪkʌ /

---

sculpter

vajar

вајар

/ vʌjʌr /

shot

kadar

кадар

/ kʌdʌr /

show

šou

шоу

/ ʃɒʊ /

show business

šou biznis

шоу бизнис

/ ʃɒʊ bɪznɪs /

silent film

nemi film

неми филм

/ nemɪ fɪlm /

singer

pevač

певач

/ pevʌtʃ /

sitcom

sitkom

ситком

/ sɪtkɒm /

---

soloist

solista

солиста

/ sɒlɪstʌ /

---

song

pesma

песма

/ pesmʌ /

---

songwriter

tekstopisac

текстописац

/ tekstɒpɪsʌts /

---

stadium

stadion

стадион

/ stʌdɪɒn /

---

stage

pozornica

позорница

/ pɒzɒrnɪtsʌ /

---

stand-up comedy

stend-ap komedija

стенд-ап комедија

/ stend-ʌp **kɒ**medɪjʌ /

television

televizija

телевизија

/ tele**vɪ**zɪjʌ /

TV show

TV šou

ТВ шоу

/ te ve ʃɒʊ /

theater

pozorište

позориште

/ **pɒ**zɒrɪʃte /

understudy

zamenik glumca

заменик глумца

/ z**ʌ**menɪk **glu**mtsʌ /

vocalist

vokal

вокал

/ v**ɒ**kʌl /

violinist

violinista

виолиниста

/ vɪɒlɪnɪstʌ /

Related verbs
Srodni glagoli
Сродни глаголи

---

to act

glumiti

глумити

/ **glʊ**mɪtɪ /

---

to applaud

aplaudirati

аплаудирати

/ ʌplaʊ**dɪr**ʌtɪ /

---

to conduct

dirigovati

дириговати

/ **dɪ**rɪgɒvʌtɪ /

---

to dance

plesati

плесати

/ **ple**sʌtɪ /

---

to direct

režirati

режирати

/ reʒɪrʌtɪ /

---

to draw

crtati

цртати

/ tsrtʌtɪ /

---

to entertain

zabavljati

забављати

/ zʌbʌvljʌtɪ /

---

to exhibit

izlagati

излагати

/ ɪzlʌgʌtɪ /

---

to host

ugostiti

угостити

/ ʊgɒstɪtɪ /

---

to paint

slikati

сликати

/ slɪkatɪ /

to perform

izvoditi

изводити

/ ɪzvɒdɪtɪ /

---

to play

igrati

играти

/ ɪgrʌtɪ /

---

to sculpt

vajati

вајати

/ vʌjʌtɪ /

---

to show

pokazati

показати

/ pɒkʌzʌtɪ /

---

to sing

pevati

певати

/ pevʌtɪ /

---

to star

glumiti

глумити

/ glʊmɪtɪ /

---

to watch

gledati

гледати

/ **gle**dʌtɪ /

TEXT – English original Orginalni Tekst na engleskom jeziku

Mark Jones is a **legend** in **show business**. His career has been nothing less than amazing. He is an award-winning **actor**, **director**, and **producer** of **film** and **television**. Jones was born in West Central, California. His mother was a teacher and his father was a police officer. He came from humble beginnings and built his career from the bottom up. As a boy, he loved to be the center of attention; he either had a **microphone** in his hand or a **guitar** over his shoulder. He was a very talented **musician** and it seemed he was headed on a path towards becoming a **singer**. He is a talented **songwriter** as well. Few people know that he released his first and only **album** when he was just 16 years old. It was a **pop album**, but It didn't have much success. That didn't stop him from finding his purpose. He also tried **stand-up comedy**. He always drew large crowds, but he knew that wasn't what he was called to do. When he was in his early twenties, he decided to try out for the local community **musical**. He was amazing in his **role** and that is when he made the decision to try acting and he has never looked back! His acting career took off fast. He got his start on a **sitcom** called *Best Friends*. That show was very popular and aired for eight full seasons. It was the beginning of Jones' long and successful and career. He went on to star in several **feature films,** such as *The Dollar, Money Maze*, and *Backyard Boys*, just to name a few. There were a few flops in his career, but that didn't stop him. He has starred in many different **genres** of films; proving his versatility as an **actor**. He has played in **dramas, comedies**, and **documentaries**. He has also won multiple major awards for his acting. As time went on, he decided to try **directing films**. He was amazing as a **director** and won awards for his work with **feature films**, such as *The Child* and *End of All*. But that wasn't enough for Mark; he became a **producer** and to no surprise, was very successful. His **films** have been wildly successful and it makes everyone wonder where he will go next. It is safe to call Mark Jones a mega-**star**. He has not only been successful in every **entertainment** venture he has attempted, he has also been successful with his family. He has been married to his wife for twenty-five years, which is a rarity in show business.

TEXT – Serbian Latin Alphabet TEKST- Srpski jezik, latinično pismo

Mark Džons je **legenda** u **šou biznisu**. Njegova karijera je ništa manje nego neverovatna. On je nagrađivani **glumac, reditelj**, i **filmski** i **televizijski producent**. Džons je rođen u Vest Centralu, Kalifornija. Njegova majka je bila učiteljica, a njegov otac je bio policajac. On je imao skromne početke i izgradio je svoju karijeru od dna ka vrhu. Kao dečak, voleo je da bude u centru pažnje; on je ili imao **mikrofon** u ruci ili **gitaru** preko ramena. Bio je veoma talentovan **muzičar** i činilo se da je bio na putu da postane **pevač**. On je, takođe, talentovan kao **tekstopisac**. Malo ljudi zna da je on izdao svoj prvi i jedini **album** kada je imao samo 16 godina. Bio je to **pop album**, ali nije imao mnogo uspeha. To ga nije sprečilo da traži svoju svrhu. On je takođe pokušao da radi i **stend-ap komedije**. Uvek je privlačio veliku masu, ali je znao da to nije ono za šta je bio stvoren da radi. Kada je bio u svojim ranim dvadesetim, on je odlučio da isproba **mjuzikl** lokalne zajednice. Bio je neverovatan u svojoj **ulozi** i tada je doneo odluku da se oproba u glumi i nikada se nije osvrtao! Njegova glumačka karijera je uzletela vrlo brzo. On je počeo sa radom u **seriji** pod nazivom Najbolji Prijatelji. Šou je bio veoma popularan i emitovan je osam punih sezona. To je bio početak Džonsove duge i uspešne karijere. On je nastavio da glumi u nekoliko **igranih filmova**, kao što su The Dollar, Money Maze, i Backyard Boys, da pomenemo samo neke. Bilo je nekoliko padova u karijeri, ali to ga nije zaustavilo. On je glumio u mnogo različitih filmskih **žanrova**; dokazujući svoju svestranost kao **glumac**. Igrao je u

dramama, **komedijama**, i **dokumentarnim filmovima**. On je takođe osvojio više značajnih nagrada za svoje uloge. Kako je vreme prolazilo, on je odlučio da pokuša **režiranje filmova**. Bio je neverovatan kao **reditelj** i osvojio je priznanja za svoj rad na **igranim filmovima**, kao što su The Child i End of All. Ali to nije bilo dovoljno za Marka; postao je **producent** i na ničije iznenađenje, bio je veoma uspešan. Njegovi **filmovi** su bili vrlo uspešni i svi se pitaju šta će biti sledeće. Slobodno možemo nazvati Marka Džonsa mega-**zvezdom**. On nije bio samo uspešan u svakom poduhvatu iz **zabavne industrije** u kojem se okušao, on je takođe bio uspešan i sa svojom porodicom. On je u braku sa suprugom dvadeset pet godina, što je retkost u šou biznisu.

TEXT – Serbian Cyrilic Alphabet TEKST- Srpski jezik, ćirilićno pismo

Марк Џонс је **легенда** у **шоу бизнису**. Његова каријера је ништа мање него неверотна. Он је награђивани **глумац**, **редитељ**, и **филмски** и **телевизијски продуцент**. Џонс је рођен у Вест Централу, Калифорнија. Његова мајка је била учитељица, а његов отац је био полицајац. Он је имао скромне почетке и изградио је своју каријеру од дна ка врху. Као дечак, волео је да буде у центру пажње; он је или имао **микрофон** у руци или **гитару** преко рамена. Био је веома талентован **музичар** и чинило се да је био на путу да постане **певач**. Он је, такође, талентован као **текстописац**. Мало људи зна да је он издао свој први и једини **албум** када је имао само 16 година. Био је то **поп албум**, али није имао много успеха. То га није спречило да тражи своју сврху. Он је такође покушао да ради и **стенд-ап комедије**. Увек је привлачио велику масу, али је знао да то није оно за шта је био створен да ради. Када је био у својим раним двадесетим, он је одлучио да испроба **мјузикл** локалне заједнице. Био је невероватан у својој **улози** и тада је донео одлуку да се опроба у глуми и никада се није осврao! Његова глумачка каријера је узлетела врло брзо. Он је почео са радом у **серији** под називом Најбољи Пријатељи. Шоу је био веома популаран и емитован је осам пуних сезона. То је био почетак Џонсове дуге и успешне каријере. Он је наставио да глуми у неколико **играних филмова**, као што су „The Dollar", „Money Maze", и „Backyard Boys", да поменемо само неке. Било је неколико падова у каријери, али то га није зауставило. Он је глумио у много различитих филмских **жанрова**; доказујћи своју свестраност као глумац. Играо је у **драмама, комедијама**, и **документарним филмовима**. Он је такође освојио више значајних награда за своје улоге. Како је време пролазило, он је одлучио да покуша **режирање филмова**. Био је невероватан као **редитељ** и освојио је признања за свој рад на **играним филмовима**, као што су „The Child" и „End of All". Али то није било довољно за Марка; постао је **продуцент** и на ничије изненађење, био је веома успешан. Његови филмови су били врло успешни и сви се питају шта ће бити следеће. Слободно можемо назвати Марка Џонса мега-**звездом**. Он није био само успешан у сваком подухвату из **забавне индустрије** у којем се окушао, он је такође био успешан и са својом породицом. Он је у браку са супругом двадесет пет година, што је реткост у шоу бизнису.

10) Games and Sports
Igre i sportovi
Игре и спортови

First Line - Vocabulary Item

Second Line - Serbian Latin

Third Line - Serbian Cyrillic

Fourth Line - Serbian Pronunciation

---

ace

as

ac

/ ʌs /

---

amateur

amater

аматер

/ ʌmʌter /

---

archery

streljaštvo

стрељаштво

/ streljʌʃtvɒ /

---

arena

arena

арена

/ ʌrenʌ /

---

arrow

strela

стрела

/ strelʌ /

---

athlete

sportista

спортиста

/ spɒrtɪstʌ /

---

badminton

badminton

бадминтон

/ bʌdmɪnton /

---

ball

lopta

лопта

/ lɒptʌ /

---

base

baza

база

/ bʌzʌ /

---

baseball

bejzbol

бејзбол

/ bejzbɒl /

---

basket

basket

баскет

/ bʌsket /

basketball

košarka

кошарка

/ kɒʃʌrkʌ /

bat

palica za bejzbol

палица за бејзбол

/ pʌlɪtsʌ zʌ bejzbɒl /

bicycle

bicikl

бицикл

/ bɪtsɪkl /

billiards

bilijar

билијар

/ bɪlɪjʌr /

bow

luk

лук

/ lʊk /

bowling

kuglanje

куглање

/ **kʊg**lʌnje /

boxing

boks

бокс

/ **bɒ**ks /

captain

kapiten

капитен

/ kʌ**pɪ**ten /

champion

šampion

шампион

/ ʃʌm**pɪ**ɒn /

championship

šampionat

шампионат

/ ʃʌmpɪ**ɒ**nʌt /

cleats

kopačke

копачке

/ **kʊ**pʌtʃke /

club

palica

палица

/ pʌlɪtsʌ /

---

competition

takmičenje

такмичење

/ tʌkmɪtʃenje /

---

course

teren

терен

/ teren /

---

court

teren

терен

/ teren /

---

cricket

kriket

крикет

/ krɪket /

---

cup

kup

куп

/ kʊp /

---

curling

karling

карлинг

/ kʌrlɪng /

---

cycling

biciklizam

бициклизам

/ bɪtsɪklɪzʌm /

---

darts

pikado

пикадо

/ pɪkʌdɒ /

---

defense

odbrana

одбрана

/ ɒdbrʌnʌ /

---

diving

ronjenje

роњење

/ rɒnjenje /

---

dodgeball

između dve vatre

између две ватре

/ ɪzmedjʊ dve vʌtre /

driver

vozač

возач

/ vɒzʌtʃ /

---

equestrian

jahač

јахач

/ jʌhʌtʃ /

---

event

događaj

догаћај

/ dɒgʌdjʌj /

---

fan

fan

фан

/ fʌn /

---

fencing

mačevanje

мачевање

/ mʌtʃevʌnje/

---

field

polje

поље

/ pɒlje /

---

figure skating

umetničko klizanje

уметничко клизање

/ ʊmetnɪtʃkɒ **klɪzʌnje** /

---

fishing

ribolov

риболов

/ **rɪbɒlɒv** /

---

football

fudbal

фудбал

/ **fʊdbʌl** /

---

game

igra

игра

/ **ɪgrʌ** /

---

gear

brzina

брзина

/ **brzɪnʌ** /

---

goal

gol

гол

/ **gɒl** /

golf

golf

голф

/ gɒlf /

golf club

palica za golf

палица за голф

/ pʌlɪtsʌ zʌ gɒlf /

gym

teretana

теретана

/ teretʌnʌ /

gymnastics

gimnastika

гимнастика

/ gɪmnʌstɪkʌ /

halftime

poluvreme

полувреме

/ pɒlʊvreme /

helmet

šlem

шлем

/ ʃlem /

hockey

hokej

хокеј

/ hɒkej /

---

horse racing

trke konja

трке коња

/ trke kɒnjʌ /

---

hunting

lov

лов

/ lɒv /

---

ice skating

skijanje na ledu

скијање на леду

/ skɪjʌnje na ledʊ /

---

inning

podela

подела

/ pɒdelʌ /

---

jockey

džokej

џокеј

/ dʒɒkej /

---

judo

džudo

џудо

/ dʒʊdɒ /

---

karate

karate

карате

/ kʌrʌte /

---

kayaking

kajak

кајак

/ kʌjʌk /

---

kickball

kikbol

кикбол

/ kɪkbɒl /

---

lacrosse

lakros

лакрос

/ lʌkrɒs /

---

league

liga

лига

/ lɪga /

---

martial arts

borilačke veštine

борилачке вештине

/ bɒrɪlʌtʃke veʃtɪne /

mat

strunjača

струњача

/ strʊnjʌtʃʌ /

match

utakmica

утакмица

/ ʊtʌkmɪtsʌ /

medal

medalja

медаља

/ medʌljʌ /

net

mreža

мрежа

/ mreʒʌ /

offense

napad

напад

/ nʌpʌd /

Olympic Games
Olimpijske Igre
Олимпијске Игре
/ ɒlɪmpɪjske ɪgre /

pentathlon
petoboj
петобој
/ petɒbɒj /

pitch
teren
терен
/ teren /

play
igra
игра
/ ɪgrʌ /

player
igrač
играч
/ ɪgrʌtʃ /

polo
polo
поло
/ pɒlɒ /

pool

bilijar

билијар

/ bɪlɪjʌr /

pool cue

štap za bilijar

штап за билијар

/ ʃtʌp za bɪlɪjʌr /

professional

profesionalac

професионалац

/ prɒfesɪɒnʌlʌts /

puck

pak

пак

/ pʌk /

quarter

četvrtina

четвртина

/ tʃetvrtɪnʌ /

race

trka

трка

/ **trk**ʌ /

race car

trkački auto

тркачки ауто

/ trkʌtʃkɪ ʌutɒ /

---

racket

reket

рекет

/ **re**ket /

---

record

izveštaj

извештај

/ ɪzveʃtʌj /

---

referee

sudija

судија

/ **s**ʊdɪjʌ /

---

relay

štafeta

штафета

/ ʃtʌ**fe**tʌ /

---

riding

jahanje

јахање

/ **j**ʌhʌnje /

---

ring

ring

ринг

/ **rɪ**ng /

---

rink

klizalište

клизалиште

/ **klɪ**zʌlɪʃte /

---

rowing

veslanje

веслање

/ **ve**slʌnje /

---

rugby

ragbi

рагби

/ **rʌ**gbɪ /

---

running

trčanje

трчање

/ **tr**tʃʌnje /

---

saddle

sedlo

седло

/ **se**dlɒ /

sailing

jedrenje

једрење

/ **je**drenje /

---

score

rezultat

резултат

/ re**zʊ**ltʌt /

---

shuffleboard

šafl tabla

шафл табла

/ **ʃ**ʌfl t**ʌ**blʌ /

---

shuttle cock

loptica za baminton

лоптица за баминтон

/ **lɒ**ptɪtsʌ zʌ **b**ʌmɪntɒn /

---

skates

klizaljke

клизаљке

/ **klɪ**zʌljke /

---

skating

klizanje

клизање

/ **klɪ**zʌnje /

---

skiing

skijanje

скијање

/ **skɪ**jʌnje /

---

skis

skije

скије

/ **skɪ**je /

---

soccer

fudbal

фудбал

/ **fʊ**dbʌl /

---

softball

softbol

софтбол

/ **sɒ**ftbɒl /

---

spectators

gledaoci

гледаоци

/ **gle**dʌɒtsɪ /

---

sport

sport

спорт

/ **spɒ**rt /

---

sportsmanship

srčanost

срчаност

/ srtʃʌnɒst /

---

squash

skvoš

сквош

/ skvɒʃ /

---

stadium

stadion

стадион

/ stʌdɪɒn /

---

surf

surfovati

сурфовати

/ sʊrfɒvʌtɪ /

---

surfboard

daska za surfovanje

даска за сурфовање

/ dʌskʌ zʌ sʊrfɒvʌnje /

---

swimming

plivanje

пливање

/ plɪvʌnje /

---

table tennis/ping pong

stoni tenis/ ping pong

стони тенис/ пинг понг

/ stɒnɪ tenɪs/ pɪng pɒng /

---

tag

privezak

привезак

/ prɪvezʌk /

---

team

tim

тим

/ tim /

---

tennis

tenis

тенис

/ tenɪs /

---

tetherball

teterbol

тетербол

/ teterbɒl /

---

throw

bacanje

бацање

/ bʌtsʌnje /

---

track

staza

стаза

/ stʌzʌ /

track and field

atletika

атлетика

/ ʌtletɪkʌ /

volleyball

odbojka

одбојка

/ ɒdbɒjkʌ /

water skiing

skijanje na vodi

скијање на води

/ skɪjʌnje na vɒdɪ /

weight lifting

dizanje tegova

дизање тегова

/ dɪzʌnje tegɒvʌ /

whistle

pištaljka

пиштаљка

/ pɪʃtʌljkʌ /

win

pobeda

победа

/ **pɒ**bedʌ /

---

windsurfing

jedrenje

једрење

/ **je**drenje /

---

winner

pobednik

победник

/ **pɒ**bednɪk /

---

wrestling

rvanje

рвање

/ **rv**ʌnje /

Related Verbs
Srodni glagoli
Сродни глаголи

to catch

uhvatiti

ухватити

/ ʊh**vʌ**tɪtɪ /

to cheat

prevariti

преварити

/ prevˈʌrɪtɪ /

to compete

takmičiti se

такмичити се

/ tˈʌkmɪtʃɪtɪ se /

to dribble

driblati

дриблати

/ drˈɪblʌtɪ /

to go

ići

ићи

/ ˈɪtjɪ /

to hit

udariti

ударити

/ ʊdˈʌrɪtɪ /

to jump

skočiti

скочити

/ skˈɒtʃɪtɪ /

to kick

udariti

ударити

/ ʊdʌrɪtɪ /

---

to knock out

nokautirati

нокаутирати

/ nɒkʌʊtɪrʌtɪ /

---

to lose

izgubiti

изгубити

/ ɪzgʊbɪtɪ /

---

to play

igrati

играти

/ ɪgrʌtɪ /

---

to race

trkati se

тркати се

/ trkʌtɪ se /

---

to run

trčati

трчати

/ trtʃʌtɪ /

---

to score

poentirati

поентирати

/ pɒentɪrʌtɪ /

---

to win

pobediti

победити

/ pɒbedɪtɪ /

TEXT – English original Orginalni Tekst na engleskom jeziku

Sports are an important part of our culture and have been throughout all history. Men specifically, are drawn to **sports** because of their competitive nature. From the time they are four or five years old, little boys are playing **sports** such as **baseball, soccer**, and **basketball**. They grow up to be men and their competitive nature grows with them. Contact **sports**, such as American **football, dodgeball, boxing, hockey**, and **wrestling** are popular among men because of their competitiveness. Women also enjoy **sports**, but usually prefer **sports** with less contact, such as **tennis, figure skating, gymnastics**, and **swimming**. In recent years, women are participating in more contact **sports** than ever before. Even retirees enjoy playing **sports, games** such as **golf** and **shuffleboard** are popular among the older crowd. Not only do people enjoy playing **sports**, they love to watch **sports** as well. Wherever you travel, you are sure to see a **fan** or two dressed in their favorite **team** colors. **Sports fan** merchandise is a huge industry. **Sports fans** spend a lot of money every year to buy **tickets** to events to cheer on their **team**. The most popular sporting **event** in the world is the **Olympic Games**. Most **athletes** dream of becoming an **Olympic medalist**. Although, there are some similarities, the **event** has changed quite a bit over the years. The **Olympics** have a rich history and began in

Greece. **Sports** played an important role in Greek culture; playing a part in religious festivals as well as used as training for the Greek military. The **Olympics** began as a festival of **sporting events** that was very popular among the people; there were over 30 thousand **spectators** in attendance. The Greeks competed in **track and field events**, such as **running, javelin, long jump, discus,** just to name a few. The also **wrestled** and had **boxing matches**. The most popular event was the **pentathlon**, which included five **events**: the **long jump, javelin, discus,** a foot **race,** and **boxing**. The **Olympic Games** and the **sports** involved have changed since that first **event**. Today's **Olympic Games** are held in a different city each year. Over 10 thousand **athletes** compete in over 300 **events!** Some of the sports in the Modern **Olympic Games** are **archery, diving, basketball, cycling, volleyball, boxing,** and the modern **pentathlon** which includes **fencing, swimming,** show jumping **(equestrian),** pistol **shooting,** and a cross country **run.**

TEXT – Serbian Latin Alphabet TEKST- Srpski jezik, latinično pismo

Sportovi su veoma bitan deo naše kulture i tako je i bilo tokom istorije. Muškarce posebno privlači **sport** zbog njihove takmičarske prirode. Od kada napune četiri ili pet godina, mali dečaci se bave sportovima kao što su **bejzbol, fudbal** i **košarka**. Oni izrastaju u muškarce i njihova takmičarska priroda raste sa njima. **Sportovi** kao što su **američki fudbal, dodžbol, boks, hokej** i **rvanje** su popularni među muškarcima zbog svog takmičarskog karaktera. Žene takođe uživaju u **sportovima,** ali obično više vole **sportove** sa manje kontakta, kao što je **tenis, umetničko klizanje, gimnastika** i **plivanje**. Poslednjih godina, žene učestvuju u više kontaktnih **sportova** nego ikada ranije. Čak i penzioneri uživaju u bavljenju **sportom,** igre kao što su **golf** ili **šaflbord** (shuffleboard) su popularne među starijima. Ne samo da ljudi uživaju u bavljenju **sportovima,** oni vole i da gledaju **sport**. Kad god putujete, možete da vidite jednog ili dva **fana** obučene u boje njihovog omiljenog **tima**. **Navijačka** roba je ogromna industrija. **Sportski** fanovi troše mnogo novca svake godine na kupovinu **karata** za **događaje** da bi navijali za svoj **tim**. Najpopularniji sportski **događaj** na svetu su **Olimpijske Igre**. Većina **sportista** sanja da dobije **Olimpijsku medalju**. Iako postoje mnoge sličnosti, ovaj događaj se promenio tokom godina. **Olimpijske igre** imaju dugu istoriju i počele su u Grčkoj. **Sportovi** su igrali bitnu ulogu u grčkoj kulturi; imali su ulogu u religijskim obredima kao i u treniranju za Grčku vojsku. **Igre** su počele kao festival **sportskih događaja** koji je bio veoma popularan među ljudima; bilo je više od 30 hiljada **gledalaca** prisutnih. Grci su se takmičili u atletskim **disciplinama**, kao što su **trke, bacanje koplja, skok u dalj, bacanje diska,** da pomenemo neke. Takođe su se **rvali** i imali **boks mečeve**. Najpopularniji događaj je bio **petoboj**, koji je uključivao pet disciplina: **skok u dalj, bacanje koplja, diska, trka,** i **boks**. **Olimpijske Igre** i sportovi su se promenili od tog prvog događaja. Danas se **Olimpijske Igre** organizuju u različitim gradovima svaki put. Preko 20 hiljada **sportista** se takmiči u preko 300 **disciplina**! Neki od sportova modernih **Olimpijskih Igara** su **streljaštvo, ronjenje, košarka, biciklizam, odbojka, boks,** i **moderni petoboj** koji uključuje **mačevanje, jahačke skokove, pucanje iz pištolja** i **atletika**.

TEXT – Serbian Cyrilic Alphabet TEKST- Srpski jezik, ćirilićno pismo

Спортови су веома битан део наше културе и тако је и било током историје. Мушкарце посебно привлачи **спорт** због њихове такмичарске природе. Од када напуне четири или пет година, мали дечаци се баве **спортовима** као што су **бејзбол, фудбал** и **кошарка**. Они израстају у мушкарце и њихова такмичарска природа расте са њима. **Спортови** као што су **амерички фудбал, доџбол, бокс, хокеј** и **рвање** су популарни међу мушкарцима због свог такмичарског карактера. Жене такође уживају у **спортовима**, али обично више воле **спортове** са мање контакта, као што је **тенис, уметничко клизање, гимнастика** и **пливање**. Последњих година, жене учествују у више контактних **спортова** него икада раније. Чак и пензионери уживају у бављењу **спортом**, игре као што су **голф** или **шафлборд** (схуффлебоард) су популарне међу старијима. Не само да људи уживају у бављењу **спортовима**, они воле и да гледају **спорт**. Кад год путујете, можете да видите једног или два **фана** обучене у боје њиховог омиљеног **тима**. **Навијачка** роба је огромна индустрија. Спортски **фанови** троше много новца сваке године на куповину **карата** за **догађаје** да би навијали за свој **тим**. Најпопуларнији спортски догађај на свету су **Олимпијске Игре**. Већина спортиста сања да добије **Олимпијску медаљу**. Иако постоје многе сличности, овај догађај се променио током година. **Олимпијске игре** имају дугу историју и почеле су у Грчкој. **Спортови** су играли битну улогу у грчкој култури; имали су улогу у религијским обредима као и у тренирању за Грчку војску. **Игре** су почеле као фестивал **спортских догађаја** који је био веома популаран међу људима; било је више од 30 хиљада **гледалаца** присутних. Грци су се такмичили у атлетским **дисциплинама**, као што су **трке**, **бацање копља, скок у даљ, бацање диска**, да поменемо неке. Такође су се **рвали** и имали **бокс мечеве**. Најпопуларнији догађај је био **петобој**, који је укључивао пет **дисциплина: скок у даљ, бацање копља, диска, трка**, и **бокс. Олимпијске Игре** и **спортови** су се променили од тог првог догађаја. Данас се **Олимпијске Игре** организују у различитим градовима сваки пут. Преко 20 хиљада **спортиста** се такмичи у преко 300 **дисциплина!** Неки од спортова модерних **Олимпијских Игара** су **стрељаштво, роњење, кошарка, бициклизам, одбојка, бокс**, и модерни **петобој** који укључује **мачевање, јахачке скокове, пуцање из пиштоља** и **атлетика**.

11) Food
Hrana
Храна

First Line - Vocabulary Item
Second Line - Serbian Latin
Third Line - Serbian Cyrillic
Fourth Line - Serbian Pronunciation

---

apple
jabuka
јабука
/ jʌbʊkʌ /

---

bacon
slanina
сланина
/ slʌnɪnʌ /

---

bagel
đevrek
ђеврек
/ djevrek /

---

banana
banana
банана
/ bʌnʌnʌ /

---

beans

pasulj

пасуљ

/ pʌsʊlj /

---

beef

govedina

говедина

/ gɒvedɪnʌ /

---

bread

hleb

хлеб

/ hleb /

---

broccoli

brokoli

броколи

/ brɒkɒlɪ /

---

brownie

kolačić

колачић

/ kɒlʌtʃitj /

---

cake

torta

торта

/ tɒrtʌ /

candy

slatkiš

слаткиш

/ slʌtkɪʃ /

---

carrot

šargarepa

шаргарепа

/ ʃʌrgʌrepʌ /

---

celery

celer

целер

/ tseler /

---

cheese

sir

сир

/ sɪr /

---

cheesecake

čizkejk

чизкејк

/ tʃɪzkejk /

---

chicken

piletina

пилетина

/ pɪletɪnʌ/

chocolate

čokolada

чоколада

/ tʃɒkɒlʌdʌ /

---

cinnamon

cimet

цимет

/ **tsɪ**met /

---

cookie

kolačić

колачић

/ kɒlʌtʃɪtj /

---

crackers

krekeri

крекери

/ **kre**kerɪ /

---

dip

umak

умак

/ ʊmʌk /

---

eggplant

plavi paradajz

плави парадајз

/ **plʌ**vɪ pʌrʌdʌjz /

fig

smokva

смоква

/ **smɒ**kvʌ /

---

fish

riba

риба

/ **rɪ**bʌ /

---

fruit

voće

воће

/ **vɒ**tje /

---

garlic

beli luk

бели лук

/ **belɪ** lʊk /

---

ginger

đumbir

ђумбир

/ **djʊ**mbɪr /

---

ham

šunka

шунка

/ **ʃʊ**nkʌ /

---

herbs

bilje

биље

/ **bɪ**lje /

---

honey

med

мед

/ **me**d /

---

ice cream

sladoled

сладолед

/ **sl**ʌdɒled /

---

jelly/jam

pekmez/džem

пекмез/џем

/ **pe**kmez/dʒem /

---

ketchup

kečap

кечап

/ **ke**tʃʌp /

---

lettuce

zelena salata

зелена салата

/ **ze**lenʌ sʌlʌtʌ /

---

mahi mahi

mahi mahi

махи махи

/ **mʌ**hɪ **mʌ**hɪ /

---

mango

mango

манго

/ **mʌ**ngɒ /

---

mayonnaise

majonez

мајонез

/ **mʌ**jonez /

---

meat

meso

месо

/ **me**sɒ /

---

melon

dinja

диња

/ **dɪ**njʌ /

---

milk

mleko

млеко

/ **mle**kɒ /

mustard

senf

сенф

/ **se**nf /

---

noodles

rezanci

резанци

/ re**zʌ**ntsɪ /

---

nuts

lešnici

лешници

/ **le**ʃnɪtsɪ /

---

oats

ovas

овас

/ **ɒ**vʌs /

---

olive

maslina

маслина

/ **mʌ**slɪnʌ /

---

orange

pomorandža

поморанџа

/ pɒ**mɒ**rʌndʒʌ /

pasta

pasta

паста

/ pʌstʌ /

---

pastry

pecivo

пециво

/ petsɪvɒ /

---

pepper

biber

бибер

/ bɪber /

---

pork

svinjetina

свињетина

/ svɪnjetɪnʌ /

---

potato

krompir

кромпир

/ krɒmpɪr /

---

pumpkin

tikva

тиква

/ tɪkvʌ /

---

raisin

suvo grožđe

суво грожђе

/ sʊvɒ grɒʒdje /

---

sage

žalfija

жалфија

/ ʒʌlfıjʌ /

---

salad

salata

салата

/ sʌlʌtʌ /

---

salmon

losos

лосос

/ lɒsɒs /

---

sandwich

sendvič

сендвич

/ sɛndvɪtʃ /

---

sausage

kobasica

кобасица

/ kɒbʌsɪtsʌ /

soup

supa

супа

/ sʊpʌ /

---

squash

bundeva

бундева

/ bʊndevʌ /

---

steak

odrezak

одрезак

/ ɒdrezʌk /

---

strawberry

jagoda

јагода

/ jʌgɒdʌ /

---

sugar

šećer

шећер

/ ʃetjer /

---

tea

čaj

чај

/ tʃʌj /

---

toast

tost

тост

/ **tɒ**st /

tomato

paradajz

парадајз

/ pʌrʌdʌjz /

vinegar

sirće

сирће

/ **sɪ**rtje /

vegetables

povrće

поврће

/ **pɒ**vrtje /

water

voda

вода

/ **vɒ**dʌ /

wheat

pšenica

пшеница

/ **pʃ**enɪtsʌ /

yogurt

jogurt

јогурт

/ **jɒ**gʊrt /

Restaurants and Cafes
Restorani i Kafići
Ресторани и Кафићи

a la carte

po narudžbini

по наруџбини

/ pɒ **nʌ**rʊdʒbɪnɪ /

---

a la mode

sa sladoledom

са сладоледом

/ sʌ **slʌ**dɒledɒm /

---

appetizer

predjelo

предјело

/ **pre**djelɒ /

---

bar

bar

бар

/ bʌr /

---

beverage

piće

пиће

/ **pɪ**tje /

---

bill

račun

рачун

/ **rʌ**tʃʊn /

---

bistro

bistro

бистро

/ **bɪ**strɒ /

---

boiled bowl

kuvana posuda

кувана посуда

/ **kʊ**vʌnʌ **pɒ**sʊdʌ /

---

braised

dinstano

динстано

/ **dɪ**nstʌnɒ /

---

breakfast

doručak

доручак

/ **dɒ**rʊtʃʌk /

---

brunch

branč

бранч

/ **br**ʌntʃ /

cafe/cafeteria

kafe

кафе

/ kʌ**fe** /

cashier

blagajnik

благајник

/ **bl**ʌgʌjnɪk /

chair

stolica

столица

/ **st**ɒlɪtsʌ /

charge

naplatiti

наплатити

/ nʌpl**ʌ**tɪtɪ /

check

račun

рачун

/ r**ʌ**tʃʊn /

chef

glavni kuvar

главни кувар

/ **glʌ**vnɪ **kʊv**ʌr /

---

coffee

kafa

кафа

/ **kʌf**ʌ /

---

coffee shop

kafić

кафић

/ **kʌf**ɪtj /

---

condiments

začini

зачини

/ **zʌ**tʃɪnɪ /

---

cook

kuvar

кувар

/ **kʊv**ʌr /

---

courses

jela

јела

/ **jel**ʌ /

---

credit card

kreditna kartica

кредитна картица

/ kredɪtnʌ kʌrtɪtsʌ /

cup

šolja

шоља

/ ʃɒljʌ /

cutlery

escajg

есцајг

/ estsʌjg /

deli/delicatessen

delikates

деликатес

/ delɪkʌtes /

dessert

dezert

дезерт

/ desert /

dine

večerati

вечерати

/ vetʃerʌtɪ /

diner

restoran

ресторан

/ restɒrʌn /

dinner

večera

вечера

/ vetʃerʌ /

dish

jelo

јело

/ jelɒ /

dishwasher

mašina za sudove

машина за судове

/ mʌʃɪnʌ zʌ sʊdɒve /

doggie bag

ostaci hrane

остаци хране

/ ɒstʌtsɪ hrʌne /

drink

piće

пиће

/ pɪtje /

entree

predjelo

предјело

/ **pre**djelɒ /

food

hrana

храна

/ **hr**ʌnʌ /

fork

viljuška

виљушка

/ **vɪ**ljʊʃkʌ /

glass

čaša

чаша

/ **tʃ**ʌʃʌ /

gourmet

sladokusac

сладокусац

/ slʌdɒ**kʊ**sʌts /

hor d'oeuvre

ordever

ордевер

/ **ɒ**rdever /

host/hostess

domaćin/domaćica

домаћин/домаћица

/ dɒmʌtjɪn/dɒmʌtjɪtsʌ /

---

knife

nož

нож

/ nɒʒ /

---

lunch

ručak

ручак

/ rʊtʃʌk /

---

maitre d'

šef

шеф

/ ʃef /

---

manager

menadžer

менаџер

/ menʌdʒer /

---

menu

meni

мени

/ menɪ /

---

mug

krigla

кригла

/ krɪglʌ /

---

napkin

salveta

салвета

/ sʌlvetʌ /

---

order

porudžbina

поруџбина

/ pɒrʊdʒbɪnʌ /

---

party

proslava

прослава

/ prɒslʌvʌ /

---

plate

tanjir

тањир

/ tʌnjɪr /

---

platter

pladanj

пладањ

/ plʌdʌnj /

---

reservation

rezervacija

резервација

/ rezervʌtsıjʌ /

---

restaurant

restoran

ресторан

/ restɒrʌn /

---

saucer

tacna

тацна

/ tʌtsnʌ /

---

server

poslužavnik

послужавник

/ pɒslʊʒʌvnɪk /

---

side order

prilog

прилог

/ prɪlɒg/

---

silverware

escajg

есцајг

/ estsʌjg /

---

special

specijalitet

специјалитет

/ spetsɪjʌlɪtet /

spoon

kašika

кашика

/ kʌʃɪkʌ /

starters

predjelo

предјело

/ **pre**djelɒ /

supper

večera

вечера

/ **ve**tʃerʌ /

table

sto

сто

/ stɒ /

tax

porez

порез

/ **pɒ**rez /

tip

napojnica

напојница

/ **nʌ**pɒjnɪtsʌ /

to go

za poneti

за понети

/ za **pɒ**netɪ /

utensils

posuđe

посуђе

/ **pɒ**sʊdje /

waiter/waitress

konobar/konobarica

конобар/конобарица

/ **kɒ**nobʌr/kɒnɒ**bʌ**rɪtsʌ /

Related verbs

Srodni glagoli

Сродни глаголи

to bake

peći

пећи

/ **pe**tjɪ /

to be hungry

biti gladan

бити гладан

/ **bɪtɪ glʌd**ʌn /

to cook

kuvati

кувати

/ **kʊvʌt**ɪ /

to cut

seći

сећи

/ **se**tjɪ /

to drink

piti

пити

/ **pɪt**ɪ /

to eat

jesti

јести

/ **je**stɪ /

to eat out

jesti vani

јести вани

/ **je**stɪ **vʌn**ɪ /

to feed

hraniti

хранити

/ hrʌnɪtɪ /

to grow

uzgajati

узгајати

/ ʊzgʌjʌtɪ /

to have breakfast

doručkovati

доручковати

/ dɒrʊtʃkɒvʌtɪ /

to have lunch

ručati

ручати

/ rʊtʃʌtɪ /

to have dinner

večerati

вечерати

/ vetʃerʌtɪ /

to make

napraviti

направити

/ nʌprʌvɪtɪ /

to order

naručiti

наручити

/ nʌrʊtʃɪtɪ /

to pay

platiti

платити

/ **pl**ʌtɪtɪ /

to prepare

pripremati

припремати

/ prɪp**rem**ʌtɪ /

to request

zahtevati

захтевати

/ zʌh**tev**ʌtɪ /

to reserve

rezervisati

резервисати

/ re**ze**rvɪsʌtɪ /

to serve

poslužiti

послужити

/ pɒs**lʊʒ**ɪtɪ /

to set the table

postaviti sto

поставити сто

/ **pɒ**stavɪtɪ st**ɒ** /

---

to taste

probati

пробати

/ **prɒ**bʌtɪ /

TEXT – English original Orginalni Tekst na engleskom jeziku

John and Mary have been dating for quite some time now. Next week is their two year anniversary and John wants to make it really special. Mary really enjoys a nice **steak dinner** out, so John is going to make **reservations** at her favorite **restaurant**. She will be so surprised because they haven't eaten there in a while and she just loves their **salad** and **bread**. John calls and speaks to the **manager** ahead of time to set up the **reservation**. Finally, the day arrives and John picks Mary up at her home. She still doesn't know where they are going, but is excited for the surprise. "Where are we going? Mary asked. "I told you, it's a surprise!" said John. So Mary begins trying to guess where their surprise destination is. "Is it our favorite **diner**? I love the laid back atmosphere and the **waitress** is so nice." "Is it the **coffee shop** on the corner? You know how much I love **coffee**." They arrive at the **restaurant** and she squeals with delight at the thought of the **cheesecake** that they serve for **dessert** . The **host** greets them at the door and promptly seats them at their favorite **table** near the **bar**. It is a quiet little corner of the **restaurant**. The server greets them, lays a **napkin** and **silverware** on their **table**, and then takes their **drink order**. She offers them an **appetizer** while they wait. When the **server** returns, she begins to tell the couple about the daily **specials**. "We'll have two of your best steak **dinners**." John said, "Nothing but the best for my girl!" They are really enjoying their **gourmet meal** and the conversation is great, as always. I think we should have **dessert** for this special night. John tells the **server** that they would like a **brownie a la mode t**o share. The server brings the delicious brownie on a **plate** with two **spoons**. John and Mary both look at the **dessert** and decide they do not have room to eat it. "I think we will need that **to-go**," said Mary. While waiting for the server to pack up their **doggie bag**, John surprised Mary by getting down on his knee to propose! The whole **restaurant** was clapping; even the **dishwasher** and **cooks** came out to congratulate the couple. What a wonderful second anniversary this turned out to be for the happy couple. Now, every year on their anniversary, they **dine** at their favorite **restaurant** to celebrate such a wonderful evening.

TEXT – Serbian Latin Alphabet TEKST- Srpski jezik, latinično pismo

Džon i Meri su već duže vremena u vezi. Sledeće nedelje je njihova druga godišnjica i Džon želi da je učini posebnom. Meri mnogo uživa u dobrom **odresku za večeru**, pa će Džon da **rezerviše** u njenom omiljenom **restoranu**. Biće veoma iznenađena jer nisu skoro bili tamo a ona voli njihovu **salatu** i **hleb**. Džonzove i razgovara sa **upravnikom** unapred da **rezerviše**. Konačno je došao taj dan i Džon odlazi po Meri kod njene kuće . Ona još uvek ne zna gde idu, ali je uzbuđena zbog iznenađenja. „Kuda idemo? Pitala je Meri. „Rekao sam ti, to je iznenađenje!" rekao je Džon. Onda je Meri počela da pogađa gde je njihova destinacija iznenađenja. „Da li je to naš omiljeni **restoran**? Sviđa mi se opuštena atmosfera i **konobarica** je vrlo fina." „Jel to **kafić** na uglu? Znaš koliko volim **kafu**." Oni dolaze u **restoran** i ona vrišti od zadovoljstva od same pomisli na **kolač sa sirom** koga služe za **dezert**. **Domaćin** ih dočekuje na vratima i brzo ih smešta za njihov omiljeni **sto** blizu **bara**. To je mali tihi ugao **restorana**. Konobarica ih pozdravlja, postavlja **salvete** i **pribor** na sto, a onda ih **pita za piće**. Nudi im **piće** dok čekaju. Kada se vratila, počinje govoriti paru o **specijalitetima** dana. „Uzećemo vaše najbolje

odreske za dvoje." Džon je rekao „Samo najbolje za moju devojku!" Oni zaista uživaju u svom **gurmanskom obroku** i razgovor je odličan, kao i uvek. Mislim da treba da uzmemo **dezert** za ovu posebnu noć. Džon kaže **konobaru** da će uzeti **kolač** da ga podele. Konobar donosi **kolač** na **tanjiru** sa dve **viljuške**. Džon i Merigledaju u **dezert** i shvataju da ne mogu više da jedu."Mislim da ćemo uzeti ovo **da ponesemo,**" rekla je Meri. Dok su čekali **konobara** da im **spakuje**, Džon je iznenadio Meri tako što se spustio na kolena da je zaprosi! Ceo **restoran** je aplaudirao; čak sui **čovek koji pere sudove** i **kuvari** izašli da čestitaju paru. Kako je ovo ispala divna druga godišnjica za srećan par. Sada, svake godine kada im je godišnjica oni **večeraju** u svom omiljenom **restoranu** da proslave tako divno veče.

TEXT – Serbian Cyrilic Alphabet TEKST- Srpski jezik, ćirilićno pismo

Џон и Мери су већ дуже времена у вези. Следеће недеље је њихова друга годишњица и Џон жели да је учини посебном. Мери много ужива у добром **одреску за вечеру**, па ће Џон да **резервише** у њеном омиљеном **ресторану**. Биће веома изненађена јер нису скоро били тамо а она воли њихову **салату** и **хлеб**. Џон зове и разговара са **управником** унапред да **резервише**. Коначно је дошао тај дан и Џон одлази по Мери код њене куће . Она још увек не зна где иду, али је узбуђена због изненађења. „Куда идемо? Питала је Мери. „Рекао сам ти, то је изненађење!" рекао је Џон. Онда је Мери почела да погађа где је њихова дестинација изненађења. „Да ли је то наш омиљени **ресторан**? Свиђа ми се опуштена атмосфера и **конобарица** је врло фина." „Јел то кафић на углу? Знаш колико волим **кафу**." Они долазе у **ресторан** и она вришти од задовољства од саме помисли на **колач са сиром** кога служе за **дезерт**. **Домаћин** их дочекује на вратима и брзо их смешта за њихов омиљени **сто** близу **бара**. То је мали тихи угао **ресторана**. **Конобарица** их поздравља, поставља **салвете** и **прибор** на **сто**, а онда их пита за **пиће**. Нуди им **пиће** док чекају. Када се вратила, почиње говорити пару о **специјалитетима** дана. „Узећемо ваше најбоље

одреске за двоје.“ Џон је рекао „Само најбоље за моју девојку!“ Они заиста уживају у свом **гурманском оброку** и разговор је одличан, као и увек. Мислим да треба да узмемо **дезерт** за ову посебну ноћ. Џон каже конобару да ће узети **колач** да га поделе. Конобар доноси **колач** на **тањиру** са две **виљушке**. Џон и Мери гледају у дезерт и схватају да не могу више да једу.“Мислим да ћемо узети ово **да понесемо**,“ рекла је Мери. Док су чекали **конобара** да им **спакује**, Џон је изненадио Мери тако што се спустио на колена да је запроси! Цео ресторан је аплаудирао; чак суи **човек који пере судове** и **кувари** изашли да честитају пару. Како је ово испала дивна друга годишњица за срећан пар. Сада, сваке године када им је годишњица они **вечерају** у свом омиљеном **ресторану** да прославе тако дивно вече.

12) Shopping
Kupovina
Куповина

First Line - Vocabulary Item

Second Line - Serbian Latin

Third Line - Serbian Cyrillic

Fourth Line - Serbian Pronunciation

---

bags

torbe

torbe

/ tɒrbe /

---

bakery

pekara

korpa

/ pekʌrʌ /

---

barcode

barkod

barkod

/ bʌr kɒd /

---

basket

korpa

pekara

/ kɒrpʌ /

---

bookstore

knjižara

knjižara

/ **knjɪʒ**ʌrʌ /

boutique

butik

butik

/ **bʊt**ɪk /

browse

gledati

gledati

/ **gled**ʌtɪ /

buggy/shopping cart

kolica za kupovinu

kolica za kupovinu

/ **kɒ**lɪtsʌ zʌ kʊpɒvɪnʊ /

butcher

mesar

mesar

/ **mes**ʌr /

buy

kupiti

kupiti

/ **kʊp**ɪtɪ /

cash

kasa

kasa

/ kʌsʌ /

cashier

kasir

kasir

/ kʌsɪr /

change

razmeniti

razmeniti

/ rʌzmenɪtɪ /

changing room

garderoba

garderoba

/ gʌrderɒbʌ /

cheap

jeftino

jeftino

/ jeftɪnɒ /

check

račun

račun

/ rʌtʃʊn /

clearance

rasprodaja

rasprodaja

/ rʌsprɒdʌjʌ /

coin

novčić

новчић

/ nɒvtʃɪtj /

convenience store

prodavnica

продавница

/ prɒdʌvnɪtsʌ /

counter

pult

пулт

/ pʊlt /

credit card

kreditna kartica

кредитна картица

/ kredɪtnʌ kʌrtɪtsʌ /

customers

mušterije

муштерије

/ mʊʃterɪje /

debit card

debitna kartica

дебитна картица

/ debɪtnʌ kartɪtsʌ /

delivery

isporuka

испорука

/ ɪspɒrʊkʌ /

department store

robna kuća

робна кућа

/ rɒbnʌ kʊtjʌ /

discount

popust

попуст

/ pɒpʊst /

discount store

diskont

дисконт

/ dɪskɒnt /

drugstore/pharmacy

apoteka

апотека

/ ʌpɒtekʌ /

electronic store

prodavnica elektronske opreme

продавница електронске опреме

/ **prɒ**dʌvnɪtsʌ **e**lektrɒnske **ɒ**preme /

---

escalator

lift

лифт

/ lɪft /

---

expensive

skupo

скупо

/ **sk**ʊpɒ /

---

flea market

buvljak

бувљак

/ **b**ʊvljʌk /

---

florist

cvećar

цвећар

/ **tsve**tjʌr /

---

grocery store

bakalnica

бакалница

/ **b**ʌkʌlnɪtsʌ /

hardware

gvožđarija

гвожђарија

/ gvɒʒdjʌrɪjʌ /

jeweler

juvelir

јувелир

/ jʊvelɪr /

mall

tržni centar

тржни центар

/ trʒni tsentʌr /

market

pijaca

пијаца

/ pɪjʌtsʌ /

meat department

mesara

месара

/ mesʌrʌ /

music store

prodavnica muzičkih instrumenata

продавница музичких инструмената

/ prɒdʌvnɪtsʌ mʊzɪtʃkɪh ɪnstrʊmenʌtʌ /

offer

ponuda

понуда

/ pɒnʊdʌ /

pet store

prodavnica ljubimaca i stvari za ljubimce

продавница љубимаца и ствари за љубимце

/ prɒdʌvnɪtsʌ ljʊbɪmʌtsʌ ɪ stvʌrɪ za ljʊbɪmtse /

purchase

kupiti

купити

/ kʊpɪtɪ /

purse

tašna

ташна

/ tʌʃnʌ /

rack

mreža za prtljag

мрежа за пртљаг

/ mreʒʌ zʌ prtljʌg /

receipt

račun

рачун

/ rʌtʃʊn /

return

povraćaj

повраћај

/ pɒvrʌtjʌj /

---

sale

rasprodaja

распродаја

/ rʌsprɒdʌjʌ /

---

sales person

prodavac

продавац

/ prɒdʌvʌts /

---

scale

vaga

вага

/ vʌgʌ /

---

size

veličina

величина

/ velɪtʃɪnʌ /

---

shelf/shelves

polica/police

полица/полице

/ pɒlɪtsʌ/pɒlɪtse /

shoe store

obućara

обућара

/ ɒbʊtjʌrʌ /

---

shop

prodavnica

продавница

/ prɒdʌvnɪtsʌ /

---

shopping center

tržni centar

тржни центар

/ trʒni tsentʌr /

---

store

radnja

радња

/ rʌdnjʌ /

---

supermarket

supermarket

супермаркет

/ sʊpermʌrket /

---

tailor

krojač

кројач

/ krɒjʌtʃ /

---

till

fioka za novac

фиока за новац

/ fɪɒkʌ zʌ **nov**ʌts /

---

toy store

prodavnica igračaka

продавница играчака

/ **pro**dʌvnɪtsʌ ɪgrʌtʃʌkʌ /

---

wallet

novčanik

новчаник

/ nɒvtʃʌnɪk /

---

wholesale

veleprodaja

велепродаја

/ veleprɒdʌjʌ /

Related Verbs
Srodni glagoli
Сродни глаголи

to buy

kupiti

купити

/ **ku**pɪtɪ /

---

to charge

naplatiti

наплатити

/ nʌplʌtɪtɪ /

---

to choose

izabrati

изабрати

/ ɪzʌbrʌti /

---

to exchange

zameniti

заменити

/ zʌmenɪtɪ /

---

to go shopping

ići u kupovinu

ићи у куповину

/ ɪtjɪ ʊ kʊpɒvɪnʊ /

---

to owe

dugovati

дуговати

/ dʊgɒvʌti /

---

to pay

platiti

платити

/ plʌtɪtɪ /

---

to prefer

više voleti

више волети

/ vɪʃe vɒletɪ /

to return

vratiti

вратити

/ vrʌtɪtɪ /

to save

sačuvati

сачувати

/ sʌtʃʊvʌtɪ /

to sell

prodati

продати

/ prɒdʌtɪ /

to shop

kupovati

куповати

/ kʊpɒvʌtɪ /

to spend

potrošiti

потрошити

/ pɒtrɒʃitɪ /

to try on

probati

пробати

/ **prɒ**bʌtɪ /

---

to want

želeti

желети

/ **ʒe**letɪ /

TEXT – English original Orginalni Tekst na engleskom jeziku

It was just a few weeks until Christmas and Mark needed to **purchase** a gift for his wife. He didn't know what he was going to get for her. First, he went to the **bookstore**, she loved to read books. He checked the **shelves** to see if he could find something she had not read before, but he had no luck with that. Then he decided to visit her favorite clothing **boutique**. The **salesperson** was very friendly and helpful as he shopped. She knew his wife and was able to help him with **sizes**. He **browsed** the **racks** for just the right gift, but he did not find anything he thought she would like. Besides, everything was so **expensive**! Next, he went to the **shoe store**. He looked around and just couldn't decide what to get for her, so he left that **store**. He resisted going to the **hardware store**, that is his favorite. He thought to himself, "I have to remember, I am **shopping** for my wife, not me!" He finally decided to go to the **mall**. There are plenty of **shops** there! As he walked through the **mall**, he was getting discouraged; he passed a couple of **department stores**, a **music store** and a **toy store**, but nothing seemed right. Finally, he came upon a **jeweler.** His wife loves jewelry. He approached the **counter** and began telling the **salesman** about his wife and the type of jewelry she wears. He was so excited to learn that the ring he picked out was on **sale**. The **salesman** told him the total and Mark reached for his **wallet** to get the **cash**. He asked the salesman, "Does that price include **tax**?" "Yes, of course", replied the **salesman**. Mark realized he didn't have enough **cash**, so he paid with his **credit card**. The salesman thanked him and gave him the ring and **receipt**. Mark was so pleased to have found a gift for his wife. He stopped by the **florist** on the way home to surprise her with some flowers. As he was leaving the **florist**, his wife called and asked him to stop by the **grocery store** on his way home. Mark decided he could get what he needed from the **convenience store**, so he stopped there, and then headed home to his wife. She was so surprised that he bought her flowers. She had a little surprise for him as well; she had stopped at the **bakery** on her way home from work. He thanked her for her thoughtful surprise. How lucky he felt to be in such a giving marriage!

TEXT – Serbian Latin Alphabet TEKST- Srpski jezik, latinično pismo

Bilo je još nekoliko nedelja do Božića i Mark je trebao da **kupi** poklon za svoju suprugu. Nije znao šta će joj uzeti. Prvo je otišao do **knjižare**, volela je da čita. Pogledao je po **policama** da vidi da li imaju nešto što ona već nije čitala, ali nije imao sreće. Onda je odlučio da poseti njen omiljeni **butik**. **Prodavačica** je bila veoma ljubazna i od velike pomoći dok je kupovao. Poznavala je njegovu suprugu i mogla je da mu pomogne oko **veličina**. **Tražio** je po **rafovima** savršeni poklon, ali nije pronašao ništa za šta je mislio da će joj se dopasti. Pored toga, sve je bilo **preskupo**! Nakon toga je otišao u **prodavnicu obuće**. Razgledao je, ali nije mogao da odluči šta da joj uzme, pa je napustio **radnju**. Suzdržao se da ne ode u **gvožđaru**, to mu je omiljena radnja. Mislio je u sebi „Moram da zapamtim, **kupujem** za ženu, ne za sebe." Napokon je odlučio da ode u **tržni centar**. Tamo ima puno **prodavnica**! Dok je koračao kroz **tržni centar**, postao je obeshrabljen, prošao je nekoliko **velikih radnji**, **muzičku prodavnicu** i **prodavnicu igračaka**, ali ništa nije delovalo dobro. Konačno je došao do **zlatara**. Njegova žena voli nakit. Prišao je **kasi** i počeo da priča **prodavcu** o svojoj ženi i vrsti nakita koji ona nosi. Oduševilo ga je to što je prsten koji je izabrao bio na **rasprodaji**. **Prodavac** mu je rekao cenu i Mark je posegao za **novčanikom** da uzme **novac**. Pitao je **prodavca** „Da li **cena** uključuje i **porez**?" „Da naravno" odgovorio je **prodavac**. Mark je shvatio da nema dovoljno **novca** pa je platio **kreditnom karticom**. Prodavac mu se zahvalio i dao mu prsten i **račun**. Mark je bio veoma zadovoljan što je pronašao poklon za svoju ženu. Svratio je i kod **cvećara** da iznenadi ženu sa cvećem. U trenutku kad je napuštao **cvećaru**, žena ga je pozvala da mu kaže da svrati do **bakalnice** na putu kući. Mark je odlučio da to može da uzme i u **običnoj prodavnici**, pa je svratio tamo, a zatim krenuo kući svojoj ženi. Bila je toliko iznenađena što joj je kupio cveće. Imala je i ona malo iznenađenje za njega. Ona je svratila u **pekaru** kad se vraćala s posla. Zahvalio joj se na lepo smišljenom iznenađenju. Kako je samo srećan što je u takvom velikodušnom braku!

TEXT – Serbian Cyrilic Alphabet TEKST- Srpski jezik, ćirilićno pismo

Било је још неколико недеља до Божића и Марк је требао да **купи** поклон за своју супругу. Није знао шта ће јој узети. Прво је отишао до **књижаре**, волела је да чита. Погледао је по **полицама** да види да ли имају нешто што она већ није читала, али није имао среће. Онда је одлучио да посети њен омиљени **бутик**. **Продавачица** је била веома љубазна и од велике помоћи док је куповао. Познавала је његову супругу и могла је да му помогне око **величина**. Тражио је по **рафовима** савршени поклон, али није пронашао ништа за шта је мислио да ће јој се допасти. Поред тога, све је било **прескупо**! Након тога је отишао у **продавницу обуће**. Разгледао је, али није могао да одлучи шта да јој узме, па је напустио **радњу**. Суздржао се да не оде у **гвожђару**, то му је омиљена **радња**. Мислио је у себи „Морам да запамтим, **купујем** за жену, не за себе." Напокон је одлучио да оде у **тржни центар**. Тамо има пуно **продавница**! Док је корачао кроз **тржни центар**, постао је обесхрабрен, прошао је неколико **великих радњи**, **музичку продавницу** и

продавницу играчака, али ништа није деловало добро. Коначно је дошао до **златара**. Његова жена воли накит. Пришао је **каси** и почео да прича **продавцу** о својој жени и врсти накита који она носи. Одушевило га је то што је прстен који је изабрао био на **распродаји**. **Продавац** му је рекао цену и Марк је посегао за **новчаником** да узме **новац**. Питао је **продавца** „Да ли **цена** укључује и **порез**?" „Да наравно" одговорио је **продавац**. Марк је схватио да нема довољно новца па је платио **кредитном картицом**. Продавац му се захвалио и дао му прстен и **рачун**. Марк је био веома задовољан што је пронашао поклон за своју жену. Свратио је и код **цвећара** да изненади жену са цвећем. У тренутку кад је напуштао **цвећару**, жена га је позвала да му каже да сврати до **бакалнице** на путу кући. Марк је одлучио да то може да узме и у **обичној продавници**, па је свратио тамо, а затим кренуо кући својој жени. Била је толико изненађена што јој је купио цвеће. Имала је и она мало изненађење за њега. Она је свратила у **пекару** кад се враћала с посла. Захвалио јој се на лепо смишљеном изненађењу. Како је само срећан што је у таквом великодушном браку!

13) At the Bank
U banci
У банци

First Line - Vocabulary Item

Second Line - Serbian Latin

Third Line - Serbian Cyrillic

Fourth Line - Serbian Pronunciation

---

account

račun

рачун

/ rʌtʃʊn /

APR/Annual Percentage Rate

godišnja stopa

годишња стопа

/ gɒdɪʃnjʌ stɒpʌ /

ATM/Automatic Teller Machine

bankomat

банкомат

/ bʌnkɒmʌt /

---

balance

saldo

салдо

/ sʌldɒ /

---

bank

banka

банка

/ bʌnkʌ /

---

bank charges

bankarska provizija

банкарска провизија

/ bʌnkʌrskʌ prɒvɪzɪjʌ /

---

bank draft

menica

меница

/ menɪtsʌ /

---

bank rate

bankarska stopa

банкарска стопа

/ bʌnkʌrskʌ stɒpʌ /

---

bank statement

bankovni izvod

банковни извод

/ bʌnkovnɪ ɪzvɒd /

---

borrower

pozajmljivač

позајмљивач

/ pɒzʌjmljɪvʌtʃ /

---

bounced check

ček bez pokrića

чек без покрића

/ tʃek bez pokrɪtjʌ /

---

cardholder

vlasnik kartice

власник картице

/ vlʌsnɪk kʌrtɪtse /

---

cash

keš

кеш

/ keʃ /

---

cashback

kešbek

кешбек

/ keʃbek /

---

check

ček

чек

/ tʃek /

---

checkbook

čekovna knjižica

чековна књижица

/ tʃekɒvnʌ knjɪʒɪtsʌ /

---

checking account

tekući račun

текући рачун

/ **te**kutjɪ **r**ʌtʃʊn /

collateral

zalog

залог

/ **z**ʌlɒg /

commission

procenat

проценат

/ **pr**ɒtsenʌt /

credit

kredit

кредит

/ **kre**dɪt /

credit card

kreditna kartica

кредитна картица

/ **kre**dɪtnʌ **k**ʌrtɪtsʌ /

credit limit

kreditni limit

кредитни лимит

/ **kre**dɪtnɪ **l**ɪmɪt /

credit rating

kreditni rejting

кредитни рејтинг

/ **kre**dɪtnɪ **rej**tɪng /

currency

valuta

валута

/ vʌ**lʊ**tʌ /

debt

dug

дуг

/ dʊg /

debit

zaduženje

задужење

/ zʌdʊ**ʒe**nje /

debit card

debitna kartica

дебитна картица

/ **de**bɪtnʌ **kʌ**rtɪtsʌ /

deposit

depozit

депозит

/ **de**pɒzɪt /

direct debit

direktno zaduženje

директно задужење

/ dɪrektnɒ zʌduʒenje /

direct deposit

dikrektan depozit

дикректан депозит

/ dɪkrektan depozɪt /

expense

trošak

трошак

/ trɒʃʌk /

fees

troškovi

трошкови

/ trɒʃkɒvɪ /

foreign exchange rate

devizni kurs

девизни курс

/ devɪznɪ kʊrs /

insurance

osiguranje

осигурање

/ ɒsɪgʊrʌnje /

interest

kamata

камата

/ kʌmʌtʌ /

Internet banking

internet bankarstvo

интернет банкарство

/ ɪnternet bʌnkʌrstvɒ /

loan

pozajmica

позајмица

/ pɒzʌjmɪtsʌ /

money

novac

новац

/ nɒvʌts /

money market

berza

берза

/ berzʌ /

mortgage

hipoteka

хипотека

/ hɪpɒtekʌ /

NSF/Insufficient Funds

nedovoljno sredstava

недовољно средстава

/ nedɒvɒljnɒ sredstʌvʌ /

online banking

onlajn bankarstvo

онлајн банкарство

/ ɒnlʌjn bʌnkʌrstvɒ /

overdraft

prekoračenje

прекорачење

/ prekɒrʌtʃenje /

payee

primalac

прималац

/ prɪmʌlʌts /

pin number

pin broj

пин број

/ pɪn brɒj /

register

registar

регистар

/ regɪstʌr /

savings account

štedni račun

штедни рачун

/ ʃtedni ratʃʊn /

statement

obračun

обрачун

/ ɒbrʌtʃʊn /

tax

porez

порез

/ pɒrez /

telebanking

telebanking

телебанкинг

/ telebʌnkɪng /

teller

blagajnik

благајник

/ blʌgʌjnɪk /

transaction

transakcija

трансакција

/ trʌnsʌktsɪjʌ /

traveler's check

putnički ček

путнички чек

/ pʊtnɪtʃkɪ tʃek /

vault

sef

сеф

/ sef/

withdraw

povući

повући

/ pɒvʊtjɪ /

Related Verbs
Srodni glagoli
Сродни глаголи

to borrow

pozajmiti

позајмити

/ pɒzʌjmɪtɪ /

to cash

iskeširati

искеширати

/ ɪskeʃɪrʌtɪ /

to charge

naplatiti

наплатити

/ nʌplʌtɪtɪ /

---

to deposit

ostaviti depozit

оставити депозит

/ ɒstʌvɪtɪ depɒzɪt /

---

to endorse

odobriti

одобрити

/ ɒdɒbrɪtɪ /

---

to enter

ući

ући

/ ʊtjɪ /

---

to hold

držati

држати

/ drʒʌtɪ /

---

to insure

osigurati

осигурати

/ ɒsɪgʊrʌtɪ /

to lend

pozajmiti

позајмити

/ pɒzʌjmɪtɪ /

to open an account

otvoriti račun

отворити рачун

/ ɒtvɒrɪtɪ rʌtʃun /

to pay

platiti

платити

/ plʌtɪtɪ /

to save

sačuvati

сачувати

/ sʌtʃʊvʌti /

to spend

potrošiti

потрошити

/ pɒtrɒʃɪtɪ /

to transfer money

izvršiti transfer novca

извршити трансфер новца

/ ɪzvrʃɪtɪ trʌnsfer nɒvtsʌ /

to withdraw

povući

повући

/ pɒvʊtjɪ /

TEXT – English original Orginalni Tekst na engleskom jeziku

If you have a job, you will probably want to open a **bank account**. The two most popular **accounts** available are **checking account** and **savings account**. **Banks** also have many other **account** options, including **credit** lines, **money market accounts, mortgages**, etc. A **checking account** is good for your day-to-day purchases and paying your bills. You usually receive a **check card**, which works similar to a **credit card** for purchases, and a **checkbook** when you open a **checking account**. Your **check card** works like a **credit card**, however it **withdraws** money directly from your **account**. **Checks** are good for paying friends and family, bills, or anytime you have to mail a payment to someone. Most merchant's accept **checks** or **check cards** for payment, so you should not have a problem with everyday purchases with your **checking account**. You can also use your **debit card** to **withdraw cash** from **ATMs**; you will need to set up a **pin number** for **ATM transactions**. Make sure you keep track of your purchases and **withdrawals** using the **check register** because you don't want to be hit with **NSF fees**. As long as you **deposit** more **money** that you take out, you will be safe from **bank fees**. Many **banks** offer **Online Bill Pay**, making it very convenient for you to pay your bills from the comfort of your home, without ever needing to purchase a stamp. Another popular **bank account** is called a **savings account**. A **savings account** is great for long term planning. **Savings accounts** pay you **interest** on the **money** in your **account**. Different **banks** offer different **interest** rates based upon your savings habits and *balance*. This is the **account** you want to put money into and only take it out in case of emergency. **Checking** and **savings accounts** work well together and are the most common types of **bank accounts** available. Many savings accounts offer **overdraft** protection for your **checking account**. If you mess up and **withdraw** too much **money**, your **savings account** funds will step in and keep you from being charged **overdraft fees**. **Banks** are a safe way to save and manage your money. There are many safeguards in place to protect your **accounts**. With so many features, such as **online bill pay, telephone banking,** and **direct deposit,** the smart and efficient way to manage your money is with a **bank account**.

TEXT – Serbian Latin Alphabet TEKST- Srpski jezik, latinično pismo

Ako imate posao, verovatno ćete želeti da otvorite **račun u banci**. Dva najpopularnija **računa** su **čekovni račun** i **štedni račun**. **Banke** imaju i mnoge druge opcije, kao što su **krediti, račune tržišta novca, hipoteke** i sl. **Čekovni račun** je dobar za svakodnevnu kupovinu i plaćanje računa. Obično se dobije **čekovna kartica** koja funkcioniše slično kao **kreditna kartica** za kupovinu i **čekovna knjižica** kada otvorite **čekovni račun**. Vaša **kartica** radi kao i **kreditna kartica**, ali ona **skida** novac direktno sa vašeg **računa**. **Čekovi** su dobri za plaćanje prijateljima i porodici, plaćanje računa ili bilo kada kad treba da pošaljete uplatu nekome. Mnogi trgovci prihvataju **čekove** ili **čekovne kartice** prilikom kupovine, pa ne biste trebali da imate problema prilikom svakodnevnih kupovina preko vaše **čekovne kartice**. Takođe možete koristiti i **debitnu karticu** da **uzimate novac** sa **bankomata**; moraćete da podesite **pin broj** za **transakcije sa bankomata**. Vodite računa da pratite svaku kupovinu i **podizanje novca** koristeći **čekovni registar** da ne biste došli u situaciju da plaćate **naknadu zbog nedovoljno novca na računu**. Sve dok budete **uplaćivali** više **novca** nego što uzimate, bićete pošteđeni **naplata banke**. Mnoge **banke** nude **plaćanje preko interneta**, zbog čega možete udobno da plaćate račune iz vaše kuće, bez potrebe da kupujete markice. Drugi popularni **račun u banci** je štedni račun. Ovaj **račun** je idealan za dugoročno planiranje. **Štedni račun** vam plaća **kamatu** na **novac** koji vam je na **računu**. Različite **banke** nude različite **kamate** u zavisnosti od učestalosti vaših plaćanja i stanja. Ovo je nalog na koji želite da uplaćujete novac i da ga podignete samo u hitnim slučajevima. **Čekovni račun** i **štedni račun** zajedno dobro funkcionišu i to su najčešći tipovi **računa** koji su zastupljeni. Mnogi štedni računi nude zaštitu od **prekoračenja** na **čekovnom računu**. Ako se pređete i **podignete** previše **novca**, vaš **štedni račun** će to pokriti i zaštititi od **naplata banke za prekoračenje**. **Banke** su siguran način da čuvate i raspolažete vašim novcem. Postoje mnoge zaštite koje čuvaju vaš novac. Sa tolikim mogućnostima, kao što su **plaćanje preko interneta**, **preko telefona**, i **direktan depozit**, pametan i efikasan način raspolaganja vašim novcem je breko **bankovnog računa**.

TEXT – Serbian Cyrilic Alphabet TEKST- Srpski jezik, ćirilično pismo

Ако имате посао, вероватно ћете желети да отворите **рачун у банци**. Два најпопуларнија **рачуна** су **чековни рачун** и **штедни рачун**. **Банке** имају и многе друге опције, као што су **кредити**, **рачуне тржишта новца**, **хипотеке** и сл. **Чековни рачун** је добар за свакодневну куповину и плаћање рачуна. Обично се добије **чековна картица** која функционише слично као **кредитна картица** за куповину и **чековна књижица** када отворите **чековни рачун**. Ваша **картица** ради као и **кредитна картица**, али она **скида** новац директно са вашег **рачуна**. **Чекови** су добри за плаћање пријатељима и породици, плаћање рачуна или било када кад треба да пошаљете уплату некоме. Многи трговци прихватају **чекове** или **чековне картице** приликом куповине, па не бисте требали да имате проблема приликом свакодневних куповина преко ваше **чековне картице**. Такође можете користити и **дебитну картицу** да **узимате новац** са **банкомата**; мораћете да подесите **пин број** за **трансакције са банкомата**. Водите рачуна да пратите сваку куповину и **подизање новца** користећи **чековни регистар** да не бисте дошли у ситуацију да плаћате **накнаду због недовољно новца на рачуну**. Све док будете **уплаћивали** више **новца** него што узимате, бићете поштеђени **наплата банке**.

Многе **банке** нуде **плаћање преко интернета**, због чега можете удобно да плаћате рачуне из ваше куће, без потребе да купујете маркице. Други популарни **рачун у банци** је **штедни рачун**. Овај **рачун** је идеалан за дугорочно планирање. **Штедни рачун** вам плаћа **камату** на **новац** који вам је на **рачуну**. Различите **банке** нуде различите **камате** у зависности од учесталости ваших плаћања и стања. Ово је налог на који желите да уплаћујете новац и да га подигнете само у хитним случајевима. **Чековни рачун** и **штедни рачун** заједно добро функционишу и то су најчешћи типови **рачуна** који су заступљени. Многи **штедни рачуни** нуде заштиту од **прекорачења** на **чековном рачуну**. Ако се пређете и **подигнете** превише **новца**, ваш **штедни рачун** ће то покрити и заштитити од **наплата банке за прекорачење**. **Банке** су сигуран начин да чувате и располажете вашим новцем. Постоје много заштите које чувају ваш новац. Са толиким могућностима, као што су **плаћање преко интернета**, **преко телефона**, и **директан депозит**, паметан и ефикасан начин располагања вашим новцем је бреко **банковног рачуна**.

14) Holidays
Praznici
Празници

First Line - Vocabulary Item
Second Line - Serbian Latin
Third Line - Serbian Cyrillic
Fourth Line - Serbian Pronunciation

balloons
baloni
балони
/ bʌlɒnɪ /

calendar
kalendar
календар
/ kʌlendʌr /

celebrate
slaviti
славити
/ slʌvɪtɪ /

celebration
proslava
прослава
/ prɒslʌvʌ /

commemorating

obeležavanje

обележавање

/ ɒbeleʒʌvʌnje /

---

decorations

ukrasi

украси

/ ʊkrʌsɪ /

---

family

porodica

породица

/ pɒrɒdɪtsʌ /

---

feast

gozba

гозба

/ gɒzbʌ /

---

federal

savezni

савезни

/ sʌveznɪ /

---

festivities

svečanosti

свечаности

/ svetʃʌnɒstɪ /

fireworks

vatromet

ватромет

/ vʌtrɒmet /

first

prvi

први

/ **pr**vɪ /

friends

prijatelji

пријатељи

/ **prɪ**jʌteljɪ /

games

igre

игре

/ ɪgre /

gifts

pokloni

поклони

/ **pɒ**klɒnɪ /

heros

heroji

хероји

/ herɒjɪ /

holiday

odmor

одмор

/ ɒdmɒr /

honor

čast

част

/ tʃʌst /

national

nacionalni

национални

/ nʌtsɪɒnʌlnɪ /

parade

parada

парада

/ pʌrʌdʌ /

party

zabava

забава

/ zʌbʌvʌ /

picnics

piknici

пикници

/ pɪknɪtsɪ /

remember

sećati se

сећати се

/ **se**tjʌtɪ se /

---

resolution

odluka

одлука

/ **ɒ**dlʊkʌ /

---

traditions

tradicije

традиције

/ **tr**ʌdɪtsɪje /

American Holidays in calendar order:
Амерички празници по календарском реду

New Year's Day

Nova godina

Нова година

/ **n**ɒvʌ **g**ɒdɪnʌ /

Martin Luther King Jr. Day

Dan Martina Lutera Kinga

Дан Мартина Лутера Кинга

/ **d**ʌn **m**ʌrtɪnʌ **l**ʊterʌ **k**ɪngʌ /

Groundhog Day

Dan mrmota

Дан мрмота

/ dʌn **mr**mɒtʌ /

Valentine's Day

Dan zaljubljenih

Дан заљубљених

/ dʌn **z**ʌljʊbljenɪh /

St. Patrick's Day

Sveti Patrik

Свети Патрик

/ **sve**tɪ **p**ʌtrɪk /

Easter

Uskrs

Ускрс

/ ʊskrs /

April Fool's Day

Prvi april

Први април

/ **pr**vɪ ʌprɪl /

Earth Day

Dan planete Zemlje

Дан планете Земље

/ dʌn plʌnete zemlje /

Mother's Day

Dan majki

Дан мајки

/ dʌn mʌjkɪ /

Memorial Day

Dan sećanja na poginule u ratu

Дан сећања на погинуле у рату

/ dʌn setjʌnjʌ nʌ pogɪnʊle ʊ rʌtʊ /

Father's Day

Dan očeva

Дан очева

/ dʌn ɒtʃevʌ /

Flag Day

Dan zastave

Дан заставе

/ dʌn zʌstʌve /

Independence Day/July 4th

Dan nezavisnosti

Дан независности

/ dʌn nezʌvɪsnostɪ /

Labor Day

Praznik rada

Празник рада

/ prʌznik rʌdʌ /

Columbus Day

Kolumbov dan

Колумбов дан

/ kɒlʊmbɒv dʌn /

Halloween

Noć veštica

Ноћ вештица

/ nɒtj veʃtɪtsʌ /

Veteran's Day

Dan veterana

Дан ветерана

/ dʌn veterʌnʌ /

Election Day

Izborni dan

Изборни дан

/ ɪzbɒrnɪ dʌn /

Thanksgiving Day

Dan zahvalnosti

Дан захвалности

/ dʌn zʌhvʌlnostɪ /

Christmas

Božić

Божић

/ bɒʒɪtj /

Hanukkah

Hanuka

Ханука

/ hʌnʊkʌ /

New Year's Eve

Novogodišnja noć

Новогодишња ноћ

/ nɒvɒgɒdɪʃnjʌ nɒtj /

Related Verbs
Srodni glagoli
Сродни глаголи

to celebrate

slaviti

славити

/ slʌvɪtɪ /

---

to cherish

negovati

неговати

/ negɒvʌtɪ /

---

to commemorate

obeležavati

обележавати

/ ɒbeleʒʌvʌtɪ /

to cook

kuvati

кувати

/ kʊvʌtɪ /

to give

dati

дати

/ dʌtɪ /

to go to

ići

ићи

/ ɪtjɪ /

to honor

poštovati

поштовати

/ pɒʃtɒvʌtɪ /

to observe

posmatrati

посматрати

/ pɒsmʌtrʌtɪ /

to party

zabavljati se

забављати се

/ zʌbʌvljʌtɪ se /

to play

igrati

играти

/ ɪɡrʌtɪ /

---

to recognize

prepoznati

препознати

/ prepɒznʌtɪ /

---

to remember

sećati se

сећати се

/ setjʌtɪ se /

---

to visit

posetiti

посетити

/ pɒsetɪtɪ /

TEXT – English original Orginalni Tekst na engleskom jeziku

Many cultures and backgrounds are represented in America. With such diversity, Americans **celebrate** many **holidays** throughout the year. There are so many **holidays** on the **calendar**, there is always something to **celebrate**. In January, **New Year's Day** is a big **celebration**, but the real celebrating comes the night before; there are **fireworks** and **parties** that are broadcast all over the world. In February, we celebrate **Valentine's Day**. It is a day that most couples express their love and affection for each other with cards and gifts. In March, we celebrate **St. Patrick's Day**. Many people wear green items and celebrate Irish heritage. **Easter** is usually celebrated in

April. It is a Christian **holiday**, but has also become a secular **holiday** celebrating the beginning of springtime. One of the most cherished **holidays** in America is **Mother's Day**. We honor and remember our mothers and grandmothers on this day; showering them with cards, gifts, and affection. Another big **holiday** in May is **Memorial Day**; originally declared as a day to remember our fallen **heroes** of the various branches of the United States military. It is now seen as the unofficial start of summertime and is celebrated with **picnics** and time with **family**. In June, we **celebrate Father's Day**, while it is not as popular as **Mother's Day**, the idea is the same; to **honor** and **remember** our fathers and grandfathers. In July we **celebrate Independence Day**, also known as **July 4th**. This is the day we **celebrate** our independence from England so many years ago. We **celebrate** with **fireworks** and **picnics** with **family** and **friends**. September brings **Labor Day**, the official end of summer. It was originally declared as a day to recognize the achievements of American workers in our economic successes. In October, we celebrate **Halloween**. Children dress up in their favorite costumes and go trick-or-treating for candy; many adults participate in the fun and have dress-up **parties**. In November, we celebrate **Thanksgiving Day**. It is a day to remember the early settlers to the new world and their achievements. We gather with **family** and **friends** to **feast** on turkey and other comfort-type foods. In December, we **celebrate Christmas Day**. **Christmas** is a Christian **holiday** that **celebrates** the birth of Jesus Christ. It is also **celebrated** by non-Christians and has many secular-type **celebrations** and **traditions**. Santa Claus visits young children on **Christmas Eve**, leaving toys and games in their stocking. **Hanukkah** is another **holiday celebrated** in December by the Jewish community; an eight-day **holiday commemorating** the rededication of the Holy Temple in Jerusalem. This is only a handful of the **holidays celebrated** by Americans. With so many **holidays**, Americans always have a reason to celebrate; so get out the **decorations**, **balloons**, and **games** and let the **festivities** begin!

TEXT – Serbian Latin Alphabet TEKST- Srpski jezik, latinično pismo

Mnoge kulture i porekla ljudi su zastupljeni u Americi. Zbog takve raznolikosti, Amerikanci **slave** različite **praznike** tokom godine. Ima toliko **praznika** u **kalendaru**, uvek postoji nešto da se slavi. U januaru, **novogodišnji dan** je velika **proslava**, ali pravo slavlje dolazi veče pre toga; održavaju se **vatromet** i **zabave** koje se prenose po celom svetu. U februaru slavimo **Dan zaljubljenih**. To je dan kada mnogi parovi iskazuju svoju ljubav i naklonost preko čestitki i poklona. U martu, slavimo **Dan Sv. Patrika**. Mnogi ljude nose nešto zeleno i slave Irsko nasleđe. **Uskrs** se obično slavi u aprilu. To je hrišćanski **praznik**, ali je takođe postao svetovni **praznik** koji slavi početak proleća. Jedan od najiščekivanijih **praznika** u Americi je **Dan majki**. Mi slavimo i sećamo se naših mama i baka na ovaj dan; obasipajući ih čestitkama, poklonima i ljubavlju. Još jedan veliki **praznik** u maju je **Dan sećanja**. Prvobitno proglašen kao dan kada se sećamo palih **heroja** iz mnogih sfera američke vojske. Danas on znači i početak leta i slavi se **izletima** i provođenjem vremena sa **porodicom**. U junu slavimo **Dan očeva**, i dok nije toliko popularan kao **Dan majki**, ideja je ista; **slavljenje** i **sećanje** na naše očeve i deke. U julu slavimo **Dan Nezavisnosti**, poznat još i kao **4.jul**. To je dan kada slavimo našu **nezavisnost** od Engleske pre mnogo godina. **Slavimo** ga uz **vatromet** i **izlete** sa **porodicom** i **prijateljima**. Septembar donosi **Praznik rada**, zvanični kraj leta. Prvobitno je zamišljen da prizna postignuća američkih radnika u našim ekonomskim uspesima. U oktobru, slavimo **Noć veštica**. Deca oblače svoje omiljene kostime i idu da prikupljaju slatkiše; mnogi odrasli učestvuju u zabavi i imaju **žurke** sa kostimima. U novembru slavimo **Dan zahvalnost**i (Thanksgiving). To je dan kada se sećamo ranih doseljenika u novi svet i njihovih postignuća. Okupljamo se sa **porodicom** i **prijateljima** gde se **jede** ćurka i druga ukusna hrana. U decembru, slavimo **Božić**. **Božić** je hrišćanski **praznik** koji slavi rođenje Isusa Hrista. **Slave** ga i ostali i sastoji se od mnogih svetovnih **proslava** i **tradicija**. Deda Mraz posećuje decu na **Badnje veče** i ostavlja igračke i igre u njihovim čarapama. **Hanuka** je još jedan **praznik** koji se **slavi** u decembru od strane jevrejske zajednice. To je osmodnevni **praznik** koji **slavi** ponovno posvećenje Svetog Hrama u Jerusalimu. Ovo su samo neki od praznika koje slave Amerikanci. Sa toliko praznika, Amerikanci uvek imaju razlog da slave; stoga iznesite **ukrase**, **balone** i **igre** i neka **slavlje** počne!

TEXT – Serbian Cyrilic Alphabet TEKST- Srpski jezik, ćirilično pismo

Многе културе и порекла људи су заступљени у Америци. Због такве разноликости, Американци **славе** различите **празнике** током године. Има толико **празника** у **календару**, увек постоји нешто да се слави. У јануару, **новогодишњи дан** је велика **прослава**, али право славље долази вече пре тога; одржавају се **ватромет** и **забаве** које се преносе по целом свету. У фебруару славимо **Дан заљубљених**. То је дан када многи парови исказују своју љубав и наклоност преко честитки и поклона. У марту, славимо **Дан Св. Патрика**. Многи људе носе нешто зелено и славе Ирско наслеђе. **Ускрс** се обично слави у априлу. То је хришћански **празник**, али је такође постао световни **празник** који слави почетак пролећа. Један од најишчекиванијх **празника** у Америци је **Дан мајки**. Ми славимо и сећамо се наших мама и бака на овај дан; обасипајући их честиткама, поклонима и љубављу. Још један велики **празник** у мају је **Дан сећања**. Првобитно проглашен као дан када се сећамо палих **хероја** из многих сфера америчке војске. Данас он значи и почетак лета и слави се **излетима** и провођењем времена са **породицом**. У јуну славимо **Дан очева**, и док није толико популаран као **Дан мајки**, идеја је иста; слављење и сећање на наше очеве и деке. У јулу славимо **Дан Независности**, познат још и као **4.јул**. То је дан када славимо нашу независност од Енглеске пре много година. Славимо га уз **ватромет** и **излете** са **породицом** и **пријатељима**. Септембар доноси **Празник рада**, званични крај лета. Првобитно је замишљен да призна постигнућа америчких радника у нашим економским успесима.

У октобру, славимо **Ноћ вештица**. Деца облаче своје омиљене костиме и иду да прикупљају слаткише; многи одрасли учествују у забави и имају журке са костимима. У новембру славимо **Дан захвалности** (Thanksgiving). То је дан када се сећамо раних досељеника у нови свет и њихових постигнућа. Окупљамо се са **породицом** и **пријатељима** где се **једе** ћурка и друга укусна храна. У децембру, славимо **Божић**. **Божић** је хришћански **празник** који слави рођење Исуса Христа. **Славе** га и остали и састоји се од многих световних **прослава** и **традиција**. Деда Мраз посећује децу на **Бадње вече** и оставља играчке и игре у њииховим чарапама. **Ханука** је још један **празник** који се слави у децембру од стране јеврејске заједнице. То је осмодневни **празник** који **слави** поновно посвећење Светог Храма у Јерусалиму. Ово су само неки од празника које славе Американци. Са толико празника, Американци увек имају разлог да славе; стога изнесите **украсе**, **балоне** и **игре** и нека **славље** почне!

15) Traveling
Putovanje
Путовање

First Line - Vocabulary Item

Second Line - Serbian Latin

Third Line - Serbian Cyrillic

Fourth Line - Serbian Pronunciation

airport

aerodrom

аеродром

/ ʌerɒdrɒm /

backpack

ranac

ранац

/ rʌnʌts /

baggage

prtljag

пртљаг

/ **pr**tljʌg /

boarding pass

karta za ukrcavanje

карта за укрцавање

/ **k**ʌrtʌ zʌ ʊkr**ts**ʌvʌnje /

business class

biznis klasa

бизнис класа

/ **bɪ**znɪs **klʌs**ʌ /

---

bus station

autobuska stanica

аутобуска станица

/ ʌʊ**tɒ**bʊskʌ **stʌ**nɪtsʌ /

---

carry-on

ručni prtljag

ручни пртљаг

/ **rʊ**tʃnɪ **pr**tljʌg /

---

check-in

prijava

пријава

/ **prɪ**jʌvʌ /

---

coach

ekonomska klasa

економска класа

/ ek**ɒnɒmsk**ʌ klʌsʌ /

---

cruise

krstarenje

крстарење

/ krstʌrenje/

---

depart/departure

poći/polazak

пођи/полазак

/ pɒtjɪ/polʌzʌk /

---

destination

odredište

одредиште

/ ɒdredɪʃte /

---

excursion

ekskurzija

екскурзија

/ ekskʊrzɪjʌ /

---

explore

istražiti

истражити

/ ɪstrʌʒɪtɪ /

---

first class

prva klasa

прва класа

/ prvʌ klʌsʌ /

---

flight

let

лет

/ let /

---

flight attendant

stjuardesa

стјуардеса

/ stjʊʌrdesʌ /

fly

leteti

летети

/ letetɪ /

guide

vodič

водич

/ vɒdɪtʃ /

highway

autoput

аутопут

/ ʌʊtɒpʊt /

hotel

hotel

хотел

/ hɒtel /

inn

krčma

крчма

/ krtʃmʌ /

journey

putovanje

путовање

/ pʊtɒvʌnje /

---

land

zemlja

земља

/ **ze**mljʌ /

---

landing

sletanje

слетање

/ **sle**tʌnje /

---

lift-off

poletanje

полетање

/ pɒ**letenje**/

---

luggage

prtljag

пртљаг

/ **pr**tljʌg /

---

map

mapa

мапа

/ **m**ʌpʌ /

---

move

pokret

покрет

/ **pɒ**kret /

---

motel

motel

мотел

/ **mɒ**tel /

---

passenger

putnik

путник

/ **pʊ**tnɪk /

---

passport

pasoš

пасош

/ **pʌ**sɒʃ /

---

pilot

pilot

пилот

/ **pɪ**lɒt /

---

port

luka

лука

/ **lʊ**kʌ /

---

postcard

razglednica

разгледница

/ rʌzglednɪtsʌ /

---

rail

pruga

пруга

/ prʊgʌ /

---

railway

pruga

пруга

/ prʊgʌ /

---

red-eye

kasan let

касан лет

/ kʌsʌn let /

---

reservations

rezervacije

резервације

/ rezervʌtsɪje /

---

resort

odmaralište

одмаралиште

/ ɒdmʌrʌlɪʃte /

---

return

povratak

повратак

/ pɒvrʌtʌk /

---

road

put

пут

/ pʊt /

---

roam

lutati

лутати

/ lʊtʌtɪ /

---

room

soba

соба

/ sɒbʌ /

---

route

ruta

рута

/ rʊtʌ /

---

safari

safari

сафари

/ sʌfʌrɪ /

---

sail

ploviti

пловити

/ plɒvɪtɪ /

---

seat

sedište

седиште

/ sedɪʃe /

---

sightseeing

razgledanje

разгледање

/ rʌzgledʌnje /

---

souvenir

suvenir

сувенир

/ sʊvenɪr /

---

step

korak

корак

/ kɒrʌk /

---

suitcase

akt tašna

акт ташна

/ ʌkt tʌʃnʌ /

take off

poleteti

полетети

/ pɒlletetɪ /

tour

tura

тура

/ tʊrʌ /

tourism

turizam

туризам

/ tʊrɪzʌm /

tourist

turista

туриста

/ tʊrɪstʌ /

traffic

saobraćaj

саобраћај

/ sʌɒbrʌtjʌj /

trek

teško putovanje

тешко путовање

/ teʃkɒ pʊtɒvʌnje /

travel

putovati

путовати

/ pʊtɒvʌtɪ /

---

travel agent

turistički agent

туристички агент

/ tʊrɪstɪtʃkɪ ʌgent /

---

trip

putovanje

путовање

/ pʊtɒvʌnje /

---

vacation

odmor

одмор

/ ɒdmɒr /

---

voyage

putovanje

путовање

/ pʊtɒvʌnje /

Modes of Transportation
Vrste prevoza
Врсте превоза

airplane/plane

avion

avion

/ ʌvɪɒn /

automobile

automobil

automobil

/ ʌʊtɒmɒbɪl /

balloon

balon

balon

/ bʌlɒn /

bicycle

bicikl

bicikl

/ bɪtsɪkl /

boat

čamac

čamac

/ tʃʌmʌts /

bus

autobus

autobus

/ ʌʊtɒbʊs /

---

canoe

kanu

kanu

/ kʌnʊ /

---

car

kola

kola

/ kɒlʌ /

---

ferry

trajekt

trajekt

/ trʌjekt /

---

motorcycle

motocikl

motocikl

/ mɒtɒtsɪkl /

---

motor home

pokretni dom

pokretni dom

/ pʊkretnɪ dɒm /

---

ship

brod

brod

/ brɒd /

---

subway

podzemna železnica

podzemna železnica

/ pɒdzemnʌ ʒeleznɪtsʌ /

---

taxi

taksi

taksi

/ tʌksɪ /

---

train

voz

voz

/ vɒz /

---

van

kombi

kombi

/ kɒmbɪ /

Hotels
Hotel
Хотел

accessible

pristupačno

приступачно

/ **prɪ**stʊpʌtʃnɒ /

---

airport shuttle

avionski prevoz

авионски превоз

/ ʌvɪɒnskɪ **pre**vɒz /

---

all-inclusive

ol inkluziv

ол инклузив

/ ɒl ɪn**klʊ**zɪv /

---

amenities

način ponašanja

начин понашања

/ **n**ʌtʃɪn pɒ**n**ʌʃʌnjʌ/

---

balcony

balkon

балкон

/ **b**ʌlkɒn /

---

bathroom

kupatilo

купатило

/ kʊpʌtɪlɒ /

beach

plaža

плажа

/ plʌʒʌ /

beds

kreveti

кревети

/ krevetɪ /

bed and breakfast

noćenje sa doručkom

нођење са доручком

/ nɒtjenje sʌ dɒrʊtʃkɒm /

bellboy/bellhop

sobar

собар

/ sɒbʌr /

bill

račun

рачун

/ rʌtʃʊn /

breakfast

doručak

доручак

/ **dɒ**rʊtʃʌk /

business center

poslovni centar

пословни центар

/ **pɒ**slɒvnɪ **tse**ntʌr /

cable/satellite tv

kablovska/satelitska

кабловска/сателитска

/ **kʌ**blɒvskʌ/sʌ**te**lɪtskʌ /

charges (in-room)

troškovi (u sobi)

трошкови (у соби)

/ **trɒ**ʃkɒvɪ (ʊ **sɒ**bi) /

check-in

prijavljivanje

пријављивање

/ prɪjʌv**ljɪ**vʌnje /

check-out

odjavljivanje

одјављивање

/ ɒdjʌv**ljɪ**vʌnje /

concierge

domar

домар

/ dɒmʌr /

Continental breakfast

kontinentalni doručak

континентални доручак

/ kɒntɪnentʌlnɪ dɒrʊtʃʌk /

---

corridors (interior)

hodnici

ходници

/ hɒdnɪtsɪ /

---

double bed

francuski krevet

француски кревет

/ frʌntsʊskɪ krevet /

---

double room

dvokrevetna soba

двокреветна соба

/ dvɒkrevetnʌ sɒbʌ /

---

elevator

lift

лифт

/ lɪft /

exercise/fitness room

soba za fitnes

соба за фитнес

/ sɒbʌ za fɪtnes /

---

extra bed

dodatni krevet

додатни кревет

/ dɒdʌtnɪ krevet /

---

floor

pod

под

/ pɒd /

---

front desk

recepcija

рецепција

/ retseptsɪjʌ /

---

full breakfast

kompletan doručak

комплетан доручак

/ kɒmpletʌn dɒrʊtʃʌk /

---

gift shop

suvenirnica

сувенирница

/ sʊvenɪrnɪtsʌ /

---

guest

gost

гост

/ gɒst /

---

guest laundry

vešernica za goste

вешерница за госте

/ veʃernɪtsʌ zʌ gɒste /

---

hair dryer

fen za kosu

фен за косу

/ fen za kɒsʊ /

---

high-rise

visoko

високо

/ vɪsɒkɒ /

---

hotel

hotel

хотел

/ hɒtel /

---

housekeeping

vođenje domaćinstva

вођење домаћинства

/ vɒdjenje dɒmʌtjɪnstvʌ /

---

information desk

info pult

инфо пулт

/ ɪnfo pʊlt /

---

inn

krčma

крчма

/ krtʃmʌ /

---

in-room

usluga u sobi

услуга у соби

/ ʊslʊga ʊ sɒbɪ /

---

internet

internet

интернет

/ ɪnternet /

---

iron/ironing board

pegla/daska za peglanje

пегла/даска за пеглање

/ peglʌ/dʌska zʌ peglʌnje /

---

key

ključ

кључ

/ kljʊtʃ /

---

king bed

veliki krevet

велики кревет

/ **ve**lɪkɪ **kre**vet /

---

lobby

lobi

лоби

/ **lɒ**bɪ /

---

local calls

lokalni pozivi

локални позиви

/ **lɒ**kʌlnɪ **pɒ**zɪvɪ /

---

lounge

čekaonica

чекаоница

/ tʃekʌɒnɪtsʌ /

---

luggage

prtljag

пртљаг

/ **pr**tljʌg /

---

luxury

luksuzno

луксузно

/ **lʊ**ksʊznɒ /

---

maid

spremačica

спремачица

/ spremʌtʃitsʌ /

manager

menadžer

менаџер

/ menʌdʒer /

massage

masaža

масажа

/ mʌsʌʒʌ /

meeting room

sala za sastanke

сала за састанке

/ sʌlʌ zʌ sʌstʌnke /

microwave

mikrotalasna

микроталасна

/ mɪkrɒtʌlʌsnʌ /

mini-bar

mini-bar

мини-бар

/ mɪnɪ-bʌr /

motel

motel

мотел

/ mɒtel /

---

newspaper

novine

новине

/ nɒvɪne /

---

newsstand

novinarnica

новинарница

/ nɒvɪnʌrnɪtsʌ /

---

non-smoking

zabranjeno pušenje

забрањено пушење

/ zʌbrʌnjenɒ pʊʃenje /

---

pets/no pets

dozvoljeni ljubimci/zabranjeni ljubimci

дозвољени љубимци/забрањени љубимци

/ dɒzvɒljenɪ ljʊbɪmtsɪ/zʌbranjenɪ ljʊbɪmtsɪ /

---

pool - indoor/outdoor

bazen – unutra/napolju

базен – унутра/напољу

/ bʌzen – ʊnʊtrʌ/nʌpɒljʊ /

porter

portir

портир

/ pɒrtɪr /

---

queen bed

veliki krevet

велики кревет

/ velɪkɪ krevet /

---

parking

parking

паркинг

/ pʌrkɪng /

---

receipt

račun

рачун

/ rʌtʃʊn /

---

reception desk

recepcija

рецепција

/ retseptsɪjʌ /

---

refrigerator (in-room)

frižider (u sobi)

фрижидер (у соби)

frɪžɪder (ʊ sɒbɪ)

---

reservation

rezervacija

резервација

/ rezervʌtsɪjʌ /

restaurant

restoran

ресторан

/ restɒrʌn /

room

soba

соба

/ sɒbʌ /

room number

broj sobe

број собе

/ brɒj sɒbe /

room service

rum servis

рум сервис

/ rʊm servɪs /

safe (in-room)

sef (u sobi)

сеф (у соби)

/ sef (ʊ sɒbɪ) /

service charge

naplata usluge

наплата услуге

/ nʌplʌtʌ ʊslʊge /

---

shower

tuš

туш

/ tʊʃ /

---

single room

jednokrevetna soba

једнокреветна соба

/ jednɒkrevetnʌ sɒbʌ /

---

suite

apartman

апартман

/ ʌpʌrtmʌn /

---

tax

porez

порез

/ pɒrez /

---

tip

napojnica

напојница

/ nʌpojnitsʌ /

twin bed

spojeni kreveti

спојени кревети

/ **spɒ**jenɪ **kre**vetɪ /

---

vacancy/ no vacancy

slobodno/zauzeto

слободно/заузето

/ **sl**ɒbɒdnɒ/**zʌ**uzetɒ /

---

wake-up call

poziv za buđenje

позив за буђење

/ **pɒ**zɪv za **bʊ**djenje /

---

whirlpool/hot tub

đakuzi

ђакузи

/ djʌ**kʊ**zɪ /

---

wireless high-speed internet

bežični internet sa brzim protokom

бежични интернет са брзим протоком

/ **be**ʒɪtʃnɪ ɪnternet sʌ **br**zɪm **prɒ**tɒkɒm /

Related Verbs
Srodni glagoli
Сродни глаголи

to arrive

stići

стићи

/ stɪtjɪ /

---

to ask

pitati

питати

/ pɪtʌtɪ /

---

to buy

kupiti

купити

/ kʊpɪtɪ /

---

to catch a flight

uhvatiti let

ухватити лет

/ ʊhvʌtɪtɪ let /

---

to change

promeniti

променити

/ prɒmenɪtɪ /

---

to drive

voziti

возити

/ **vɒ**zɪtɪ /

---

to find

naći

наћи

/ **nʌ**tjɪ /

---

to fly

leteti

летети

/ **le**tetɪ /

---

to land

sleteti

слетети

/ **sle**tetɪ /

---

to make a reservation

rezervisati

резервисати

/ rezer**vɪs**ʌtɪ /

---

to pack

pakovati

паковати

/ **pʌ**kɒvʌtɪ /

---

to pay

platiti

платити

/ pl**ʌ**tɪtɪ /

---

to recommend

preporučiti

препоручити

/ prepɒ**rʊ**tʃɪtɪ /

---

to rent

iznajmiti

изнајмити

/ ɪzn**ʌ**jmɪtɪ /

---

to see

videti

видети

/ **vɪ**detɪ /

---

to stay

ostati

остати

/ ɒst**ʌ**tɪ /

---

to take off

uzleteti

узлетети

/ ʊz**le**tetɪ /

---

to travel

putovati

путовати

/ pʊtɒvʌtɪ /

---

to swim

plivati

пливати

/ plɪvʌtɪ /

TEXT – English original Orginalni Tekst na engleskom jeziku

Michael is young and adventurous and loves to **travel**; ever since he was a little boy, he has enjoyed the excitement of **traveling**. Whether he **travels** by **boat, car,** or **plane**; he always has a great time. Michael has **traveled** all over the world on **vacation**. Once, he took a **bus** from Florida to California, just to say he had done so. His wife enjoys **traveling** with Michael; however, she is not an adventurous person. She likes to **vacation** in nice, quiet places. She prefers an easy **trip** that does not require **layovers** or complicated **itineraries**. Her favorite **destination** is Hawaii, so Michael decided to take her there for their anniversary. They made their **reservations** and took a **plane** from California to Hawaii; or so they thought. That is where this **journey** begins. They bought **tickets** on the **red-eye flight** to get an early start on **vacation**. They arrived at the **airport**, got their **luggage checked-in** and with their **carry-on bags** in hand, they headed towards the **concourse**, ready to **fly** away into the sunset! They were in such a hurry to get to their **destination**; they unknowingly **boarded** the wrong **plane**. They both slept during the **flight** and when they arrived, they both felt something was not quite right; they had traveled to **Alaska**! They checked with their **travel agency** and found out there were no **flights** leaving that **airport** until the next morning. Determined to get to their **vacation** in

Hawaii, the couple decided to do whatever it took to get there! They took a **ferry** to the nearest **car** rental location and decided to **drive** as much of the way as possible; they would figure the rest out later. They picked up a **map** and headed on their way. They figured they would get to do some **sightseeing** along the way, if nothing else. It was a long **drive**; they drove for hundreds of miles until they just couldn't drive anymore, so they stopped at a **hotel** to get some rest. The next morning, they **checked-out** of their **hotel room** and continued driving. Their **travel agent** called them and said that they had **coach tickets** the next morning, leaving out of LAX **airport**; they just had to be there in time. The couple made it to the **airport** with just ten minutes to spare! They finally **boarded** their **flight**, on their way to Hawaii. When they arrived at the **airport**, they were so relieved to finally be on **vacation**! They took a **shuttle** to the **resort** and finally were able to enjoy a nice, relaxing **vacation**. Of all Michael's **travels**, this was the most adventurous one yet!

TEXT – Serbial Latin Alphabet TEKST- Srpski jezik, latinično pismo

Majkl je mlad i avanturista i voli da **putuje**; Od kada je bio mali dečak uživa u uzbuđenjima **putovanja**. Bilo da putuje **čamcem**, **automobilom**, ili **avionom**, on se uvek odlično provede. Majkl je **putovao** širom sveta na **odmor**. Jednom je išao **autobusom** od Floride do Kalifornije, samo da kaže da je to uradio. Njegova žena uživa da **putuje** s njim; međutim, ona nije avanturističkog duha. Voli da ide na **odmor** na lepa, mirna mesta. Ona voli više laka **putovanja** koja ne uključuju **prekide putovanja** i komplikovane **rasporede**. Njena omiljena **destinacija** su Havaji, pa je Majkl odlučio da je tamo odvede za godišnjicu. **Rezervisali** su **let** i otišli iz Kalifornije na Havaje; ili su bar tako mislili. Tu **putovanje** i počinje. Kupili su **karte** za **noćni let** kako bi rano ujutru počeli sa **odmorom**. Stigli su na **aerodrom**, **prijavili prtljag** i sa **ručnim prtljagom** u rukama išli ka **holu**, spremni da **odlete** u zalazak sunca! Bili su u tolikoj žurbi da odu na svoje **odredište**, da su se ne znajuci **ukrcali** na pogrešan **avion**. Oboje su spavali tokom **puta**, i kada su stigli osetili su da nešto nije u redu; otišli su na **Aljasku**! Proverili su sa svojom **agencijom** i saznali da nema nijednog **leta** do sutra ujutru. Odlučni da odu na **odmor** na Havaje, par je odlučio da uradi sve što treba da odu tamo! Uzeli su **trajekt** do najbližeg centra za iznajmljivanje **automobila** i odlučili da **voze** koliko god im put dozvoljava; za ostatak će se snaći kasnije. Uzeli su **mapu** i krenuli na put. Shvatili su da će, ako ništa drugo, bar **razgledati** okolinu dok putuju. Bila je to duga **vožnja**. Vozili su stotinama milja, sve dok više nisu mogli, pa su stali u jedan **hotel** da se odmore. Sledećeg jutra, **odjavili** su se iz **hotela** i nastavili sa vožnjom. Njihov **agent** ih je pozvao i rekao da imaju **karte** za sledeće jutro, da polaze sa **aerodroma** LAX, samo moraju da budu tamo na vreme. Par je uspeo da stigne za deset minuta na **aerodrom**! Konačno su se **ukrcali** na **avion** za Havaje. Kada su stigli na **aerodrom**, bilo im je lakše jer su konačno bili na **odmoru**! **Autobusom** su otišli do **odmarališta** i konačno su mogli da uživaju u lepom, opuštajućem **odmoru**. Od svih Majklovih **putovanja**, ovo je bilo najuzbudljivije od svih!

TEXT – Serbial Cyrilic Alphabet TEKST- Srpski jezik, ćirilićno pismo

Мајкл је млад и авантуриста и воли да **путује**; Од када је био мали дечак ужива у узбуђењима **путовања**. Било да путује **чамцем**, **аутомобилом**, или **авионом**, он се увек одлично проведе. Мајкл је **путовао** широм света на **одмор**. Једном је ишао **аутобусом** од Флориде до Калифорније, само да каже да је то урадио. Његова жена ужива да **путује** с њим; међутим, она није авантуристичког духа. Воли да иде на **одмор** на лепа, мирна места. Она воли више лака **путовања** која не укључују **прекиде путовања** и компликоване **распореде**. Њена омиљена **дестинација** су Хаваји, па је Мајкл одлучио да је тамо одведе за годишњицу. **Резервисали** су **лет** и отишли из Калифорније на Хаваје; или су бар тако мислили. Ту **путовање** и почиње. Купили су **карте** за **ноћни лет** како би рано ујутру почели са **одмором**. Стигли су на **аеродром**, **пријавили пртљаг** и са **ручним пртљагом** у рукама ишли ка **холу**, спремни да **одлете** у залазак сунца! Били су у толикој журби да оду на своје **одредиште**, да су се не знајући **укрцали** на погрешан **авион**. Обоје су спавали током **пута**, и када су стигли осетили су да нешто није у реду; отишли су на **Аљаску**! Проверили су са својом **агенцијом** и сазнали да нема ниједног **лета** до сутра ујутру. Одлучни да оду на **одмор** на Хаваје, пар је одлучио да уради све што треба да оду тамо! Узели су **трајект** до најближег центра за изнајмљивање **аутомобила** и одлучили да **возе** колико год им пут дозвољава; за остатак ће се снаћи касније. Узели су **мапу** и кренули на пут. Схватили су да ће, ако ништа друго, бар **разгледати** околину док путују. Била је то дуга **вожња**. Возили су стотинама миља, све док више нису могли, па су стали у један **хотел** да се одморе. Следећег јутра, **одјавили** су се из **хотела** и наставили са вожњом. Њихов **агент** их је позвао и рекао да имају **карте** за следеће јутро, да полазе са **аеродрома** ЛАХ, само морају да буду тамо на време. Пар је успео да стигне за десет минута на **аеродром**! Коначно су се **укрцали** на **авион** за Хаваје. Када су стигли на **аеродром**, било им је лакше јер су коначно били на **одмору**! **Аутобусом** су отишли до **одмаралишта** и коначно су могли да уживају у лепом, опуштајућем **одмору**. Од свих Мајклових **путовања**, ово је било најузбудљивије од свих!

16) School
Škola
Школа

First Line - Vocabulary Item

Second Line - Serbian Latin

Third Line - Serbian Cyrillic

Fourth Line - Serbian Pronunciation

---

arithmetic

aritmetika

аритметика

/ ʌrɪtmetɪkʌ /

---

assignment

zadatak

задатак

/ zʌdʌtʌk /

---

atlas

atlas

атлас

/ ʌtlʌs /

---

backpack

ranac

ранац

/ rʌnʌts /

---

binder

povezivač

повезивач

/ pɒvezɪvʌtʃ /

blackboard

tabla

табла

/ tʌblʌ /

book

knjiga

књига

/ **knjig**ʌ /

bookbag

ranac za knjige

ранац за књиге

/ rʌnʌts zʌ **knjɪ**ge /

bookcase

polica za knjige

полица за књиге

/ pɒlɪtsʌ zʌ **knjɪ**ge /

bookmark

obeleživač stranica

обележивач страница

/ ɒbeleʒɪvʌtʃ **strʌ**nɪtsʌ /

calculator

digitron

дигитрон

/ **dɪ**gɪtrɒn /

---

calendar

kalendar

календар

/ kʌlendʌr /

---

chalk

kreda

креда

/ **kre**dʌ /

---

chalkboard

tabla

табла

/ tʌblʌ /

---

chart

grafikon

графикон

/ grʌ**fɪ**kɒn /

---

class clown

razredni klovn

разредни кловн

/ rʌzrednɪ **klɒ**vn /

---

classmate

drug iz razreda

друг из разреда

/ drʊg ɪz rʌzredʌ /

classroom

učionica

учионица

/ ʊtʃɪɒnɪtsʌ /

clipboard

fascikla

фасцикла

/ fʌstsɪklʌ /

coach

trener

тренер

/ trener kɒlʌ /

colored pencils

drvene bojice

дрвене бојице

/ drvene bɒjɪtse /

compass

kompas

компас

/ kɒmpʌs /

composition book

vežbanka

вежбанка

/ **ve**ʒbʌnkʌ /

computer

kompjuter

компјутер

/ kɒmp**ju**ter /

construction paper

građevinski papir

грађевински папир

/ **gr**ʌdjevɪnskɪ **p**ʌpɪr /

crayons

masne bojice

масне бојице

/ **m**ʌsne **b**ɒjɪtse /

desk

klupa

клупа

/ kl**u**pʌ /

dictionary

rečnik

речник

/ **re**tʃnɪk /

diploma

diploma

диплома

/ dɪplɒmʌ /

---

dividers

separatori

сепаратори

/ sepʌrʌtɒrɪ /

---

dormitory

spavaonica

спаваоница

/ spʌvʌɒnɪtsʌ /

---

dry-erase board

tabla

табла

/ tʌblʌ /

---

easel

štafelaj

штафелај

/ ʃtʌfelʌj /

---

encyclopedia

enciklopedija

енциклопедија

/ entsɪklɒpedɪjʌ /

---

english

engleski

енглески

/ ˈɛnglɛskɪ /

---

eraser

gumica

гумица

/ ˈɡʊmɪtsʌ /

---

exam

ispit

испит

/ ˈɪspɪt /

---

experiment

eksperiment

експеримент

/ ɛkspɛrɪˈmɛnt /

---

flash cards

fleš kartice

флеш картице

/ fleʃ ˈkʌrtɪtse /

---

folder

folder

фолдер

/ ˈfɒldɛr /

---

geography

geografija

географија

/ geɒgrʌfɪjʌ /

globe

globus

глобус

/ **glɒ**bʊs /

glossary

glosar

глосар

/ **glɒ**sʌr /

glue

lepak

лепак

/ **le**pʌk /

gluestick

lepak

лепак

/ **le**pʌk /

grades, A, B, C, D, F, passing, failing

ocene, A, B, C, D, F, prolaz, pada

оцене, А, Б, Ц, Д, Ф, пролаз, пада

/ **ɒ**tsene, ʌ, b, ts, d, f, **prɒ**lʌz, **pʌ**dʌ /

gym

teretana

теретана

/ teretʌnʌ /

headmaster

upravnik

управник

/ ʊprʌvnɪk /

highlighter

marker

маркер

/ mʌrker /

history

istorija

историја

/ ɪstɒrɪjʌ /

homework

domaći

домаћи

/ dɒmʌtjɪ /

ink

mastilo

мастило

/ mʌstɪlɒ /

janitor

domar

домар

/ dɒmʌr /

Kindergarten

obdanište

обданиште

/ ɒbdʌnɪʃte /

---

keyboard

tastatura

тастатура

/ tʌstʌtʊrʌ/

---

laptop

laptop

лаптоп

/ lʌptɒp /

---

lesson

lekcija

лекција

/ lektsɪjʌ /

---

library

biblioteka

библиотека

/ bɪblɪɒtekʌ /

librarian

bibliotekar

библиотекар

/ bɪblɪɒtekʌr /

---

lockers

ormarići

ормарићи

/ ɒrmʌrɪtjɪ /

---

lunch

ručak

ручак

/ rʊtʃʌk /

---

lunch box/bag

torbica za užinu

торбица за ужину

/ tɒrbɪtsʌ zʌ ʊʒɪnʊ /

---

map

mapa

мапа

/ mʌpʌ /

---

markers

markeri

маркери

/ mʌrkerɪ /

---

math

matematika

математика

/ mʌtemʌtɪkʌ /

notebook

sveska

свеска

/ sveskʌ /

notepad

beležnica

бележница

/ beleʒnɪtsʌ /

office

kancelarija

канцеларија

/ kʌntselʌrɪjʌ /

paper

papir

папир

/ pʌpɪr /

paste

zalepiti

залепити

/ zʌlepɪtɪ /

pen

hemijska olovka

хемијска оловка

/ **he**mɪjskʌ ɒlɒvkʌ /

---

pencil

obična olovka

обична оловка

/ **ɒ**bɪtʃnʌ ɒlɒvkʌ /

---

pencil case

futrola

футрола

/ fʊtrɒlʌ /

---

pencil sharpener

rezač

резач

/ **re**zʌtʃ /

---

physical education/PE

fizičko

физичко

/ **fɪ**zɪtʃkɒ /

---

portfolio

portfolio

портфолио

/ pɒrt**fɒ**lɪɒ /

---

poster

poster

постер

/ pɒster /

---

principal

upravnik

управник

/ ʊprʌvnɪk /

---

professor

profesor

професор

/ prɒfesɒr /

---

project

projekat

пројекат

/ prɒjekʌt /

---

protractor

uglomer

угломер

/ ʊglɒmer /

---

pupil

đak

ђак

/ djʌk /

---

question

pitanje

питање

/ pɪtʌnje /

---

quiz

kviz

квиз

/ kvɪz /

---

read

čitati

читати

/ tʃɪtʌtɪ /

---

reading

čitanje

читање

/ tʃɪtʌnje /

---

recess

odmor

одмор

/ ɒdmɒr /

---

ruler

lenjir

лењир

/ lenjɪr /

---

science

nauka

наука

/ nʌʊkʌ /

---

scissors

makaze

маказе

/ mʌkʌze /

---

secretary

sekretarica

секретарица

/ sekretʌrɪtsʌ /

---

semester

polugodište

полугодиште

/ pɒlʊgɒdɪʃte /

---

stapler

heftalica

хефталица

/ heftʌlɪtsʌ /

---

student

učenik

ученик

/ ʊtʃenɪk /

---

tape

traka

трака

/ trʌkʌ /

teacher

nastavnik

наставник

/ nʌstʌvnɪk /

test

test

тест

/ test /

thesaurus

tezaurus

тезаурус

/ tezʌʊrus /

vocabulary

rečnik

речник

/ retʃnɪk /

watercolors

vodene boje

водене боје

/ vɒdene bɒje /

whiteboard

tabla

табла

/ tʌblʌ /

---

write

pisati

писати

/ pɪsʌtɪ /

Related Verbs
Srodni glagoli
Сродни глаголи

---

to answer

odgovoriti

одговорити

/ ɒdgɒvɒrɪtɪ /

---

to ask

pitati

питати

/ pɪtʌtɪ /

---

to draw

crtati

цртати

/ tsrtʌtɪ /

to drop out

ispasti

испасти

/ ɪspʌstɪ /

---

to erase

obrisati

обрисати

/ ɒbrɪsʌtɪ /

---

to fail

pasti

пасти

/ pʌstɪ /

---

to learn

naučiti

научити

/ nʌʊtʃɪtɪ /

---

to pass

položiti

положити

/ pɒlɒʒɪtɪ /

---

to play

igrati

играти

/ ɪgrʌtɪ /

---

to read

čitati

читати

/ tʃɪtʌtɪ /

to register

registrovati

регистровати

/ regɪstrɒvʌtɪ /

to show up

pojaviti se

појавити се

/ pɒjʌvɪtɪ se /

to sign up

prijaviti se

пријавити се

/ prɪjʌvɪtɪ se /

to study

učiti

учити

/ ʊtʃɪtɪ /

to teach

predavati

предавати

/ predʌvʌtɪ /

to test

testirati

тестирати

/ testɪrʌtɪ /

---

to think

misliti

мислити

/ mɪslɪtɪ /

TEXT – English original Orginalni Tekst na engleskom jeziku

Heather is five years old and has always enjoyed being home with her mom every day. She heard that she would be starting **school** soon and was nervous about it. Summer was coming to an end and Heather was really starting to get anxious about the start of the **school** year. This will be her first and she is unsure about what to expect. She was excited, yet nervous to leave her mom all day. Her mom took her **school supply** shopping on the Saturday before school was to start. She had her list of **school supplies** and was very overwhelmed by all the things in the store. There are so many things on the list, she doesn't know where to start; **crayons**, **paper**, **markers**, **glue**, and more! Heather's mom told her she would need something to put all this stuff in, so she picked out a nice **backpack** with her favorite cartoon cat on it; it also had a matching **lunch bag**! Her mom told her she would also need to get some new clothes because every little girl needs new clothes for the first day of **school**. On the way home from shopping, Heather questioned her mom about **school;** she was getting very excited because she wondered what she would be doing with all this stuff! The first day of **school** finally came and Heather's mom took her to register for the first day of **Kindergarten**. The first stop was the **office**, she met a very nice lady, the **school secretary**, and she also met a handsome gentleman who said he was the **principal** of the **school**. She wasn't sure what that meant, but he must be important. Once everything was settled in the **office**, her mom took her to her new **classroom**. When she walked in, she couldn't believe her eyes; it was amazing! There was a big **chalkboard** on the wall, rows of **desks**, colorful **charts** and **maps**, even some games and **books**. She really likes games and **books**, so she started to relax a bit. Then, she saw her new **teacher**; she was a nice lady, smiling and being very polite. Heather then realized she would be okay. She sent her mom on her way and told her she would see her this afternoon after **school.** She was ready to learn to **read** and **write**, do **math** and **science**; she was not nervous anymore! That day she made several new friends and really like her **teacher**. They had **English** and **Math**; she even got to paint using her new **watercolors**. Heather decided she loved **school** and wanted to come back every day!

TEXT – Serbian Latin Alphabet TEKST- Srpski jezik, latinično pismo

Heder ima pet godina i oduvek je uživala da bude kući sa svojom mamom svakog dana. Čula je da će uskoro da počne da ide u **školu** i bila je veoma nervozna zbog toga. Leto se bližilo kraju i Heder je počela da bude veoma uplašena zbog početka **školske** godine. Ovo će joj biti prva godina i ne zna šta da očekuje. Bila je uzbuđena ali nervozna što će ostaviti mamu celi dan. Njena mama je odvela u kupovinu **potrepština za školu** u subotu pre nego što je škola trebala da počne. Imala je spisak **potrepština za školu** i bila je previše uzbuđena zbog svega šta se nalazilo u prodavnici. Bilo je toliko stvari na spisku, nije znala gde da počne; **bojice**, **papir**, **flomasteri**, **lepak** i mnogo toga! Hederina mama joj je rekla da će joj trebati nešto gde će staviti sve te stvari pa je izabrala lep **ranac** sa njenom omiljenom macom iz crtanih filmova; imala je istu takvu **torbicu za ručak**! Mama joj je isto rekla da joj je potrebna nova odeća zato što svakoj maloj devojčici treba nova odeća za prvi dan **škole**. U povratku kući iz kupovine, Heder je ispitivala mamu o **školi**; bila je veoma uzbuđena jer se pitala šta sve može da uradi sa svim ovim stvarima! Prvi dan **škole** je konačno došao i mama je odvela Heder da se upiše u **obdanište**. Prvo su otišle u **kancelariju**, upoznala je veoma dobru ženu, **sekretara škole**, i takođe je upoznala veoma lepog gospodina koji je rekao da je **direktor škole**. Nije bila sigurna šta to znači, ali je sigurno bilo nešto važno. Kada je sve bilo sređeno u **kancelariji**, mama je odvela u njenu novu **učionicu**. Kada je ušla, nije mogla da veruje; bilo je predivno! Tamoje bila velika **tabla** na zidu, redovi **klupa**, **panoi** i **mape** u različitim bojama, čak i neke igre i **knjige**. Ona zaista voli igre i **knjige**, pa se malo opustila. Onda, videla je svoju novu **učiteljicu**; bila je to jedna dobra žena, koja se osmehivala i bila veoma ljubazna. Heder je onda shvatila da će biti u redu. Ispratila je majku i rekla da će se videti tog popodneva posle **škole**. Bila je spremna da nauči da **čita** i **piše**, radi **matematiku i nauku**; više nije bila nervozna! Tog dana je upoznala nekoliko novih prijatelja i zavolela svoju novu **učiteljicu**. Imali su **engleskii matematiku**; čak je mogla i da boji koristeći svoje **vodene boje**. Heder je odlučila da voli **školu** i da želi da se vraća ovde svaki dan.

TEXT – Serbian Cyrilic Alphabet TEKST- Srpski jezik, ćirilićno pismo

Хедер има пет година и одувек је уживала да буде кући са својом мамом сваког дана. Чула је да ће ускоро да почне да иде у **школу** и била је веома нервозна због тога. Лето се ближило крају и Хедер је почела да буде веома уплашена због почетка **школске** године. Ово ће јој бити прва година и не зна шта да очекује. Била је узбуђена али нервозна што ће оставити маму цели дан. Њена мама је одвела у куповину **потрпштина за школу** у суботу пре него што је школа требала да почне. Имала је списак **потрепштина за школу** и била је превише узбуђена због свега шта се налазило у продавници. Било је толико ствари на списку, није знала где да почне; **бојице**, **папир**, **фломастери**, лепак и много тога! Хедерина мама јој је рекла да ће јој требати нешто где ће ставити све те ствари па је изабрала леп **ранац** са њеном омиљеном мацом из цртаних филмова; имала је исту такву

торбицу за ручак! Мама јој је исто рекла да јој је потребна нова одећа зато што свакој малој девојчици треба нова одећа за први дан **школе**. У повратку кући из куповине, Хедер је испитивала маму о школи; била је веома узбуђена јер се питала шта све може да уради са свим овим стварима! Први дан **школе** је коначно дошао и мама је одвела Хедер да се упише у **обданиште**. Прво су отишле у канцеларију, упознала је веома добру жену, **секретара школе**, и такође је упознала веома лепог господина који је рекао да је **директор школе**. Није била сигурна шта то значи, али је сигурно било нешто важно. Када је све било сређено у канцеларији, мама је одвела у њену нову **учионицу**. Када је ушла, није могла да верује; било је предивно! Тамоје била велика **табла** на зиду, редови **клупа**, **панои** и **мапе** у различитим бојама, чак и неке игре и **књиге**. Она заиста воли игре и **књиге**, па се мало опустила. Онда, видела је своју нову **учитељицу**; била је то једна добра жена, која се осмехивала и била веома љубазна. Хедер је онда схватила да ће бити у реду. Испратила је мајку и рекла да ће се видети тог поподнева после **школе**. Била је спремна да научи да **чита** и **пише**, ради **математику** и **науку**; више није била нервозна! Тог дана је упознала неколико нових пријатеља и заволела своју нову **учитељицу**. Имали су **енглескии математику**; чак је могла и да боји користећи своје **водене боје**. Хедер је одлучила да воли **школу** и да жели да се враћа овде сваки дан.

17) Hospital
Bolnica
Болница

First Line - Vocabulary Item
Second Line - Serbian Latin
Third Line - Serbian Cyrillic
Fourth Line - Serbian Pronunciation

---

ache
bol
бол
/ bɒl /

---

acute
akutno
акутно
/ ʌkʊtnɒ /

---

allergy/allergic
alergija/alergičan
алергија/алергичан
/ ʌlergɪjʌ/ʌlergɪtʃʌn /

---

ambulance
hitna pomoć
хитна помоћ
/ hɪtnʌ pɒmɒtj /

---

amnesia

amnezija

амнезија

/ ʌmnezɪjʌ /

---

amputation

amputacija

ампутација

/ ʌmpʊtʌtsɪjʌ /

---

anaemia

anemija

анемија

/ ʌnemɪjʌ /

---

anesthesiologist

anesteziolog

анестезиолог

/ ʌnestezɪɒlɒg /

---

antibiotics

antibiotici

антибиотици

/ ʌntɪbɪɒtɪtsɪ /

---

anti-depressant

antidepresiv

антидепресив

/ ʌntɪdepresɪv /

appointment

sastanak

састанак

/ sʌstʌnʌk /

arthritis

artritis

артритис

/ ʌrtrɪtɪs /

asthma

astma

астма

/ ʌstmʌ /

bacteria

bakterija

бактерија

/ bʌkterɪjʌ /

bedsore

dekubitus

декубитус

/ dekʊbɪtus /

biopsy

biopsija

биопсија

/ bɪɒpsɪjʌ /

blood

krv

крв

/ krv /

blood count

krvna slika

крвна слика

/ krvnʌ slɪkʌ /

blood donor

donator krvi

донатор крви

/ dɒnʌtɒr krvɪ /

blood pressure

krvni pritisak

крвни притисак

/ krvnɪ prɪtɪsʌk /

blood test

test krvi

тест крви

/ tɛst krvɪ /

bone

kost

кост

/ kɒst /

brace

kopča

копча

/ kɒptʃʌ /

---

bruise

modrica

модрица

/ mɒdrɪtsʌ /

Caesarean section (C-section)

carski rez

царски рез

/ tsʌrskɪ rez /

---

cancer

rak

рак

/ rʌk /

---

cardiopulmonary

kardiopulmonalna

кардиопулмонална

/ kʌrdɪɒpʊlmɒnʌlnʌ /

---

resuscitation (CPR)

veštačko disanje

вештачко дисање

/ veʃtatʃkɒ dɪsʌnje /

case

slučaj

случај

/ slʊtʃʌj /

cast

gips

гипс

/ gɪps /

chemotherapy

hemoterapija

хемотерапија

/ hemɒterʌpijʌ /

coroner

islednik

иследник

/ ɪslednɪk /

critical

kritično

критично

/ krɪtɪtʃnɒ /

crutches

štake

штаке

/ ʃtʌke /

cyst

cista

циста

/ **ts**ɪstʌ /

---

deficiency

nedostatak

недостатак

/ nedɒst**ʌ**tʌk /

---

dehydrated

dehidriran

дехидриран

/ de**h**ɪdrɪrʌn /

---

diabetes

dijabetes

дијабетес

/ dɪj**ʌbe**tes /

---

diagnosis

dijagnoza

дијагноза

/ dɪjʌgnɒzʌ /

---

dietician

dijetičar

дијетичар

/ dɪ**je**tɪtʃʌr /

---

disease

bolest

болест

/ **bɒ**lest /

---

doctor

doktor

доктор

/ **dɒ**ktɒr /

---

emergency

hitan slučaj

хитан случај

/ **hɪ**tʌn **slʊ**tʃʌj /

---

emergency room (ER)

urgentni centar

ургентни центар

/ ʊr**ge**ntnɪ tsentʌr/

---

exam

pregled

преглед

/ **pre**gled /

---

fever

groznica

грозница

/ **grɒ**znɪtsʌ /

flu (influenza)

prehlada

прехлада

/ **pre**hlʌdʌ /

---

fracture

prelom

прелом

/ **pre**lɒm /

---

heart attack

srčani napad

срчани напад

/ srtʃʌnɪ **nʌ**pʌd /

---

hematologist

hematolog

хематолог

/ hemʌ**tɒ**log /

---

hives

koprivnjača

копривњача

/ kɒp**rɪ**vnjʌtʃʌ /

---

hospital

bolnica

болница

/ **bɒ**lnɪtsʌ /

---

illness

bolest

болест

/ bɒlest /

---

imaging

slikanje

сликање

/ slɪkʌnje /

---

immunization

imunizacija

имунизација

/ ɪmʊnɪzʌtsɪjʌ /

---

infection

infekcija

инфекција

/ ɪnfektsɪjʌ /

Intensive Care Unit (ICU)

intenzivna nega

интензивна нега

/ ɪntenzɪvnʌ negʌ /

IV

intravenski

интравенски

/ ɪntrʌvenskɪ /

laboratory (lab)

laboratorija

лабораторија

/ lʌbɒrʌtɒrɪjʌ /

---

life support

održavanje života

одржавање живота

/ ɒdrʒʌvʌnje ʒɪvɒtʌ /

---

mass

masa

маса

/ mʌsʌ /

---

medical technician

medicinski tehničar

медицински техничар

/ medɪtsɪnskɪ tehnɪtʃʌr /

---

neurosurgeon

neurohirurg

неурохирург

/ neʊrɒhɪrʊrg /

---

nurse

medicinska sestra

медицинска сестра

/ medɪtsɪnskʌ sestrʌ /

operating room (OR)

operaciona sala

операциона сала

/ ɒperʌtsɪɒnʌ sʌlʌ /

---

operation

operacija

операција

/ ɒperʌtsɪjʌ /

---

ophthalmologist

oftalmolog

офталмолог

/ ɒftʌlmɒlɒg /

---

orthopedic

ortoped

ортопед

/ ɒrtɒped /

---

pain

bol

бол

/ bɒl /

---

pediatrician

pedijatar

педијатар

/ pedɪjʌtʌr /

pharmacist

farmaceut

фармацеут

/ fʌrmʌtseʊt /

---

pharmacy

apoteka

апотека

/ ʌpɒtekʌ /

---

physical Therapist

fizioterapeut

физиотерапеут

/ fɪzɪɒterʌpeʊt /

---

physician

lekar

лекар

/ lekʌr /

---

poison

otrov

отров

/ ɒtrɒv /

---

prescription

recept

рецепт

/ retsept /

---

psychiatrist

psihijatar

психијатар

/ psɪhɪjʌtʌr /

---

radiologist

radiolog

радиолог

/ rʌdɪɒlɒg /

---

resident

specijalizant

специјализант

/ specɪjʌlɪzʌnt /

---

scan

skeniranje

скенирање

/ skenɪrʌnje/

---

scrubs

stažisti

стажисти

/ stʌʒɪstɪ /

---

shots

snimci

снимци

/ snɪmtsɪ /

---

side effects

neželjeni efekti

нежељени ефекти

/ **ne**ʒeljenɪ efektɪ /

---

specialist

specijalista

специјалиста

/ spetsɪjʌlɪstʌ /

---

stable

stabilno

стабилно

/ **st**ʌbɪlnɒ /

---

surgeon

hirurg

хирург

/ **h**ɪrʊrg /

---

symptoms

simptomi

симптоми

/ sɪmptɒmɪ /

---

therapy

terapija

терапија

/ terʌpɪjʌ /

---

treatment

lečenje

лечење

/ letʃenje /

vein

vena

вена

/ venʌ /

visiting hours

vizita

визита

/ vɪzɪtʌ /

visitor

posetilac

посетилац

/ pɒsetɪlʌts /

wheelchair

kolica

колица

/ kɒlɪtsʌ /

x-ray

rendgen

рендген

/ rendgen /

Related Verbs
Srodni glagoli
Сродни глаголи

to bring

doneti

донети

/ **dɒ**netɪ /

to cough

kašljati

кашљати

/ **kʌ**ʃjʌtɪ /

to examine

ispitati

испитати

/ ɪs**pɪ**tʌtɪ /

to explain

objasniti

објаснити

/ ɒb**jʌ**snɪtɪ /

to feel

osećati

осећати

/ ɒ**se**tjʌtɪ /

to give

dati

дати

/ **d**ʌtɪ/

---

to hurt

povrediti

повредити

/ pɒ**vred**ɪtɪ /

---

to prescribe

prepisati

преписати

/ pre**pɪs**ʌtɪ /

---

to scan

skenirati

скенирати

/ ske**nɪr**ʌtɪ /

---

to take

uzeti

узети

/ ʊzetɪ /

---

to test

testirati

тестирати

/ te**stɪr**ʌtɪ /

to treat

lečiti

лечити

/ letʃɪtɪ /

---

to visit

posetiti

посетити

/ pɒsetɪtɪ /

---

to wait

čekati

чекати

/ tʃekʌtɪ /

---

to x-ray

snimiti

снимити

/ snɪmɪtɪ /

TEXT – English original Orginalni Tekst na engleskom jeziku

James was a happy, **healthy** ten year old boy who loved sports and riding his bike; but one day that all came to a halt. James had been complaining that his back was hurting. The **pain** was so bad one morning; he couldn't even get out of bed. His mom decided to take him to the **emergency room** to get **examined** by a **doctor**. The **nurses** were very friendly and their number one priority was making sure James was not in **pain** and could rest comfortably. The **doctor** decided to order an **x-ray** of his back. The **radiologist** read the report; he and the **ER doctor** agreed that James had an unknown **mass** on his spine. James was immediately admitted to the **hospital** for **blood tests**. The **blood tests** did not reveal the cause of the **mass,** so the **pediatrician** overseeing his **case** decided he needed some more extensive **imaging tests,** as well as a **biopsy.** James was nervous because so many **doctors** were coming to see him; an **orthopedic doctor,** a **neurosurgeon,** and a **hematologist.** The **nurses** did a good job at keeping his mind at ease. They brought him movies and video games to play to keep him busy. He had many **visitors;** friends and family members came to see him. He loved the visits with the **therapy** dogs the most; they were such comforting and sweet dogs. They had so many activities and fun for the **patients** at the children's **hospital.** James was a real trooper when they had to take **blood** and put his **IV** in his arm. James spent twelve days in the **hospital** before they finally **diagnosed** him with a **bone infection.** The **physical therapist** fit him with a back brace and he was **prescribed antibiotics.** After undergoing multiple **blood tests,** **image scans,** and a **biopsy,** James was ready to go home. He was not able to do the normal things other kids could do because of the damage to his spine, but he was so happy to be home with his family and on the mend from his terrible back **infection.** After several months of **treatment** and spinal **surgery** to straighten his back, James is now a strong, healthy, and happy boy. Through it all; the **treatments, tests, hospital** stays, and **therapy,** James has been an inspiration and hero to many who walked this journey with him.

TEXT – Serbian Latin Alphabet TEKST- Srpski jezik, latinično pismo

Džejms je bio srećan, **zdrav** desetogodišnji dečak koji je voleo sport i vožnju biciklom; ali jednog dana sve je to prestalo. Džejms je počeo da se žali na bolove u leđima. **Bol** je bila toliko jaka da jednog jutra nije mogao čak ni da ustane iz kreveta. Njegova majka je odlučila da ga odvede u **urgentni centar** da ga **doktor pregleda. Medicinske sestre** su bile veoma prijatne i najbitnija stvar za njih bila je da Džejms nema **bolove** i da se odmara. **Doktor** je odlučio da uradi **rendgen** njegove kičme. **Radiolog** je pročitao izveštaj; on i **doktor** su se složili da Džejms ima nepoznatu izraslinu na kičmi. Džejms je odmah primljen u **bolnicu** zbog **testova krvi**. **Testovi** nisu otkrili uzrok te **izrasline**, tako da je **pedijatar** koji je pratio njegov **slučaj** odlučio da mu je potrebno uraditi još neka opširnija dijagnostička **snimanja**, kao i **biopsiju**. Džejms je bio nervozan zbog toga što je mnogo **doktora** dolazilo da ga vidi; **ortoped**, **neurohirurg**, i **hematolog**. **Sestre** su dobro uradile svoj posao i on je bio smiren. Donele su mu filmove i video igre da ima šta da radi. Imao je mnogobrojne **posetioce**; prijatelji i članovi porodice su dolazili da ga vide. Najviše je voleo posete **terapijskih** pasa, bili su tako utešnii slatki psi. Imali su mnogo aktivnosti i zabave za **pacijente** u dečijoj **bolnici**. Džejms je bio baš hrabar kada su morali da mu uzmu **krv** i stave **braunilu** u ruku. Džejms je morao da provede dvanaest dana u **bolnici** dok su konačno **ustanovili** da je dobio **infekciju kosti**. **Fizioterapeut** mu je namestio protezu za kičmu i bili su mu **prepisani antibiotici**. Nakon što je obavio mnogobrojne **testove krvi**, **snimanja** i **biopsiju**, Džejms je bio spreman da ide kući. Nije mogao da radi normalne stvari koje rade ostala deca, zbog oštećenja kičme, ali je bio srećan što je ponovo sa porodicom i da se oporavlja od užasne **infekcije**. Posle nekoliko meseci lečenja i operacije kičme kako bi se ispravila njegova leđa, Džejms je sad jak, zdrav i srećan dečak. Kroz sve što je prošao: lečenje, testove, boravak u bolnici, terapiju, Džejms je bio inspiracija i heroj mnogima koji su bili uz njega sve vreme.

TEXT – Serbian Cyrilic Alphabet TEKST- Srpski jezik, ćirilično pismo

Џејмс је био срећан, **здрав** десетогодишњи дечак који је волео спорт и вожњу бициклом; али једног дана све је то престало. Џејмс је почео да се жали на болове у леђима. **Бол** је била толико јака да једног јутра није могао чак ни да устане из кревета. Његова мајка је одлучила да га одведе у **ургентни центар** да га **доктор прегледа**. **Медицинске сестре** су биле веома пријатне и најбитнија ствар за њих била је да Џејмс нема **болове** и да се одмара. **Доктор** је одлучио да уради **рендген** његове кичме. **Радиолог** је прочитао извештај; он и **доктор** су се сложили да

Џејмс има непознату **израслину** на кичми. Џејмс је одмах примљен у **болницу** због **тестова крви**. **Тестови** нису открили узрок те **израслине**, тако да је **педијатар** који је пратио његов **случај** одлучио да му је потребно урадити још нека опширнија дијагностичка **снимања**, као и **биопсију**. Џејмс је био нервозан због тога што је много **доктора** долазило да га види; **ортопед**, **неурохирург**, и **хематолог**. **Сестре** су добро урадиле свој посао и он је био смирен. Донеле су му филмове и видео игре да има шта да ради. Имао је многобројне **посетиоце**; пријатељи и чланови породице су долазили да га виде. Највише је волео посете **терапијских** паса, били су тако утешнии слатки пси. Имали су много активности и забаве за **пацијенте** у дечијој **болници**. Џејмс је био баш храбар када су морали да му узму **крв** и ставе **браунилу** у руку. Џејмс је морао да проведе дванаест дана у **болници** док су коначно и **установили** да је добио **инфекцију кости**. **Физиотерапеут** му је наместио протезу за кичму и били су му **преписани антибиотици**. Након што је обавио многобројне **тестове крви**, **снимања** и **биопсију**, Џејмс је био спреман да иде кући. Није могао да ради нормалне ствари које раде остала деца, због оштећења кичме, али је био срећан што је поново са породицом и да се опоравља од ужасне **инфекције**. После неколико месеци лечења и операције кичме како би се исправила његова леђа, Џејмс је сад јак, здрав и срећан дечак. Кроз све што је прошао: лечење, тестове, боравак у болници, терапију, Џејмс је био инспирација и херој многима који су били уз њега све време.

18) Emergency
Hitan slučaj
Хитан случај

First Line - Vocabulary Item
Second Line - Serbian Latin
Third Line - Serbian Cyrillic
Fourth Line - Serbian Pronunciation

---

accident
nesreća
несрећа
/ nesretjʌ /

---

aftershock
posledica
последица
/ pɒsledɪtsa/

---

ambulance
kola hitne pomoći
кола хитне помоћи
/ kɒlʌ hɪtne pɒmɒtjɪ /

---

asthma attack
napad astme
напад астме
/ nʌpʌd ʌstme /

---

avalanche

lavina

лавина

/ lʌvinʌ /

---

blizzard

mećava

међава

/ metjʌvʌ /

---

blood/bleeding

krv/krvarenje

крв/крварење

/ krv/krvʌrenje /

---

broken bone

slomljena kost

сломљена кост

/ slɒmljenʌ kɒst /

---

car accident

saobraćajka

саобраћајка

/ sʌɒbrʌtjʌjkʌ /

---

chest pain

bol u grudima

бол у грудима

/ bɒl u grʊdimʌ /

choking
davljenje
давЉење
/ dʌvljenje /

coast guard
obalska straža
обалска стража
/ ɒbʌlskʌ strʌʒʌ /

crash
sudar
судар
/ sʊdʌr /

diabetes
dijabetes
дијабетес
/ dɪjʌbetes /

doctor
doktor
доктор
/ dɒktɒr /

drought
suša
суша
/ sʊʃʌ /

drowning

davljenje

давељење

/ **d**ʌvljenje /

earthquake

zemljotres

земљотрес

/ **ze**mljɒtres /

emergency

hitna pomoć

хитна помоћ

/ **hɪ**tnʌ **pɒ**mɒtj /

emergency services

usluge hitne pomoći

услуге хитне помоћи

/ **ʊ**sluge **hɪ**tne **pɒ**mɒtjɪ /

EMT (emergency medical technician)

medicinski tehničar u u hitnoj pomoći

медицински техничар у хитној помоћи

/ **me**dɪtsɪnskɪ **te**hnɪtʃʌr ʊ **hɪ**tnɒj **pɒ**mɒtjɪ /

explosion

eksplozija

експлозија

/ **e**ksplɒzɪjʌ /

fight

tuča

туча

/ tʊtʃʌ /

fire

vatra

ватра

/ vʌtrʌ /

fire department

vatrogasna služba

ватрогасна служба

/ vʌtrɒgʌsnʌ slʊʒbʌ /

fire escape

požarne stepenice

пожарне степенице

/ pɒʒʌrne stepenɪtse /

firefighter

vatrogasac

ватрогасац

/ vʌtrɒgʌsʌts /

fire truck

vatrogasna kola

ватрогасна кола

/ vʌtrɒgʌsnʌ kɒlʌ /

first aid

prva pomoć

прва помоћ

/ prvʌ pɒmɒtj /

---

flood

poplava

поплава

/ pɒplʌvʌ /

---

fog

magla

магла

/ mʌglʌ /

---

gun

pištolj

пиштољ

/ pɪʃtɒlj /

---

gunshot

pucanj

пуцањ

/ pʊtsʌnj /

---

heart attack

srčani napad

срчани напад

/ srtʃʌnɪ nʌpʌd /

heimlich maneuver

Hajmlikov zahvat

Хајмликов захват

/ hʌjmlɪkɒv zʌhvʌt /

help

pomoć

помоћ

/ pɒmɒtj /

hospital

bolnica

болница

/ bɒlnɪtsʌ /

hurricane

uragan

ураган

/ ʊrʌgʌn /

injury

povreda

повреда

/ pɒvredʌ /

ladder

merdevine

мердевине

/ merdevɪne /

lifeguard

spasilac

спасилац

/ spʌsɪlʌts /

---

life support

Održavanje života

Одржавање живота

/ ɒdrʒʌvʌnje ʒɪvɒtʌ /

---

lightening

sevanje

севање

/ sevʌnje /

---

lost

izgubljen

изгубљен

/ ɪzgʊbljen /

---

mudslide

odron

одрон

/ ɒdrɒn /

---

natural disaster

prirodna katastrofa

природна катастрофа

/ prɪrɒdnʌ kʌtʌstrɒfʌ /

nurse

medicinska sestra

медицинска сестра

/ medɪtsɪnskʌ sestrʌ /

officer

policajac

полицајац

/ pɒlɪtsʌjʌts /

paramedic

bolničar

болничар

/ bɒlnɪtʃʌr /

poison

otrov

отров

/ ɒtrɒv /

police

policija

полиција

/ pɒlɪtsɪjʌ /

police car

policijski auto

полицијски ауто

/ pɒlɪtsɪjskɪ ʌʊtɒ /

rescue

spašavanje

спашавање

/ spʌʃʌvʌnje /

robbery

pljačka

пљачка

/ **plj**ʌtʃkʌ /

shooting

pucnjava

пуцњава

/ **p**ʊtsnjʌvʌ /

stop

stop

стоп

/ stɒp /

storm

oluja

олуја

/ ɒlʊjʌ /

stroke

moždani udar

мождани удар

/ **m**ɒʒdʌnɪ ʊdʌr /

temperature

temperatura

температура

/ temperʌtʊrʌ /

thief

lopov

лопов

/ lɒpɒv /

tornado

tornado

торнадо

/ tɒrnʌdɒ /

tsunami

cunami

цунами

/ tsʊnʌmi /

unconscious

bez svesti/onesvešćen

без свести/онесвешћен

/ bez svestɪ/ɒнесвеʃtjeн /

weather emergency

vremenska nepogoda

временска непогода

/ vremenskʌ nepɒgɒdʌ/

Related Verbs
Srodni glagoli
Сродни глаголи

to bleed

krvariti

крварити

/ krvʌriti /

---

to break

polomiti

поломити

/ pɒlɒmiti /

---

to breathe

disati

дисати

/ disʌti /

---

to burn

izgoreti

изгорети

/ izgɒreti /

---

to call

pozvati

позвати

/ pɒzvʌti /

---

to crash

slomiti

сломити

/ **slɒ**mɪtɪ /

to cut

iseći

исећи

/ ɪ**se**tjɪ /

to escape

izbegnuti

избегнути

/ ɪz**beg**nʊtɪ /

to faint

onesvestiti se

онесвестити се

/ ɒnes**ve**stɪtɪ se /

to fall

pasti

пасти

/ **p**ʌstɪ /

to help

pomoći

помоћи

/ pɒ**mɒ**tjɪ /

to hurt

povrediti

повредити

/ pɒvredɪtɪ /

to rescue

spasiti

спасити

/ spʌsɪtɪ /

to save

sačuvati

сачувати

/ sʌtʃʊvʌtɪ /

to shoot

upucati

упуцати

/ ʊpʊtsʌtɪ /

to wheeze

krkljati

кркљати

/ krkljʌtɪ /

to wreck

slomiti

сломити

/ slɒmɪtɪ /

TEXT – English original Orginalni Tekst na engleskom jeziku

One of the most important things parents can teach their children is how to handle an **emergency**. You often hear stories on the news about a child who saved someone by making a wise decision in an **emergency**. What you don't hear are the stories when children made a poor decision. Unfortunately, many children would not know what to do in case of a real **emergency** such as a **fire**, a **flood**, or if a parent had a **heart attack**. We hope that our children are never put in these situations, but we want them to be prepared. In an **emergency**, such as a **tornado**, an **earthquake**, or other **natural disaster**, children might react in two very dangerous ways; one of which is the superhero reaction. In this case, children think they can "save the day" and play **rescue** worker. They might try to run into a burning building or swim out to save someone in a **flood**. Make sure your children know that there are people such as **firefighters**, **police officers**, and EMTs that are professionally trained to handle these situations. It may seem safe to "**help**", but the danger may not be obvious to a child. If they try to "**help**" in a dangerous situation, it may make the **emergency** worse! The best thing to do is call **emergency services** and they will tell you exactly what you can do to **help**. On the other hand, the opposite reaction can be just as dangerous. Some children will try to run and hide from scary situations. Even though you may be scared, try to remain calm, find a phone, and call for **help**. As I said earlier, children often play a big role in the **rescue** efforts during an **emergency**. Here are some practical tips to teach your children about **emergency** situations. 1) Take a deep breath, relax and look around for **help**. 2) Call for **help**; either by yelling or phone. If someone has an **injury** or are hurt, the **rescue** workers can be there fast. In a **life threatening** situation, the **emergency operator** can often walk you through step-by-step what to do. 3) Never hang up on the operator; they will need details about your location and the **emergency** situation. 4) Find a safe place to wait for help. Do not put yourself in danger while you wait for the professionals, it will only create a bigger **emergency**. The best way to handle an **emergency** is to prepare yourself for one. If you know what to do in different **emergencies**, you will be better equipped to handle them. Ask your parents to teach you the **fire escape** plan in your home or what to do in case someone is **injured** at home. Ask someone to show you how to call for help; make sure the phone numbers for the **fire department**, **police**, and **ambulance** service numbers are posted on your home phone. As you get older, you can even take a **first aid** class. Remember, in all **emergencies**, remain calm and call for help and never put yourself in danger.

TEXT – Serbian Latin Alphabet TEKST- Srpski jezik, latinično pismo

Jedna od najbitnijih stvari koju roditelji mogu da nauče svoju decu je kako da se snađu u **hitnim slučajevima**. Često se na vestima čuju priče o detetu koje je uspelo da spase nekoga tako što je donelo mudru odluku u nekom **hitnom slučaju**. Ono što ne čujemo su priče kada su deca donela lošu odluku. Nažalost, mnoga deca ne bi znala šta da rade u slučaju prave **nesreće** kao što su **požar, poplava**, ili kada bi roditelj imao **srčani napad**. Mi se nadamo da se naša deca nikad neće naći u ovakvim situacijama, ali želimo da budu spremni. U **hitnom slučaju,** kao što je **tornado, zemljotres**, ili neka druga **prirodna nepogoda**, deca mogu da reaguju na dva veoma opasna načina; jedna od njih je reakcija super heroja. U ovom slučaju, dete misli da može da spasi situaciju i izigrava **spasioca**. Mogu da pokušaju da utrče u zapaljenu zgradu ili da otplivaju da spase nekoga iz poplavi. Postarajte se da vaša deca znaju da postoje ljudi kao što su **vatrogasci, policajci i medicinski radnici** koji su profesionalno obučeni da se nose sovakvim situacijama. Može da izgleda sigurno da se **pomogne**,ali opasnost može biti nevidljiva detetu. Ako pokušaju "**da pomognu**" u **hitnom slučaju**, to može čak i da je pogorša! Najbolje što može da se uradi je da se pozove **služba za hitne slučajeve** i oni će vam reći tačno šta treba da radite da biste **pomogli**. Na drugoj strani, reakcija suprotna ovoj može biti podjednako opasna. Neka deca će pokušati da beže i da se sakriju od opasne situacije. Iako možete da budete uplašeni, pokušajte da ostanete smireni, nađite telefon i pozovite **pomoć**. Kao što sam ranije rekao, deca često igraju veliku ulogu u pokušaju **spašavanja** tokom **hitnog slučaja**. Evo nekoliko praktičnih saveta kako danaučite decu o hitnim slučajevima. 1) Duboko udahnite, opustite se i pokušajte da nađete **pomoć**. 2) Pozovite **pomoć**; ili dozivanjem ili telefonom. Ako neko ima **ranu** ili je povređen, **spasilačke** ekipe mogu brzo da stignu. U situaciji **opasnoj po život**, **operater** može da vam da postepeno uputstvo šta da radite. 3) Nikada ne prekidajte vezu operateru; trebaju im svi detalji o vašoj trenutnoj lokaciji i **situaciji** u kojoj se nalazite. 4) Nađite sigurno mesto gde ćete čekati pomoć. Ne dovodite sebe u opasnost dok čekate profesionalce, to će samo napraviti još veću **opasnost**. Najbolji način da se snađete u **opasnoj situaciji** je da budete spremni za nešto tako. Ako znate šta da radite u različitim **situacijama**, bićete spremniji da se suočite sa njima. Pitajte roditelje šta da radite u slučaju **požara** u kući ili ako je neko iz kuće **povređen**. Pitajte nekoga da vam pokaže kako da pozovete pomoć; postarajte se da brojevi telefona **vatrogasne službe, policije, hitne pomoći** budu memorisani u vašem telefonu. Kako budete stariji, možete i da krenete na časove **prve pomoći**. Zapamtite, u bilo kojoj **opasnosti**, ostanite smireni i pozovite pomoć i ne dovodite sebe u opasnost.

TEXT – Serbian Cyrilic Alphabet TEKST- Srpski jezik, ćirilično pismo

Једна од најбитнијих ствари коју родитељи могу да науче своју децу је како да се снађу у **хитним случајевима**. Често се на вестима чују приче о детету које је успело да спасе некога тако што је донело мудру одлуку у неком **хитном случају**. Оно што не чујемо су приче када су деца донела лошу одлуку. Нажалост, многа деца не би знала шта да раде у случају праве **несреће** као што су **пожар, поплава**, или када би родитељ имао **срчани напад**. Ми се надамо да се наша деца никад неће наћи у оваквим ситуацијама, али желимо да буду спремни. У **хитном случају**, као што је **торнадо, земљотрес**, или нека друга **природна непогода**, деца могу да реагују на два веома опасна начина;

једна од њих је реакција супер хероја. У овом случају, дете мисли да може да спаси ситуацију и изиграва **спасиоца**. Могу да покушају да утрче у запаљену зграду или да отпливају да спасе некога из поплави. Постарајте се да ваша деца знају да постоје људи као што су **ватрогасци, полицајци и медицински радници** који су професионално обучени да се носе соваквим ситуацијама. Може да изгледа сигурно да се **помогне**,а ли опасност може бити невидљива детету. Ако покушају "**да помогну**" у **хитном случају**, то може чак и да је погорша! Најбоље што може да се уради је да се позове **служба за хитне случајеве** и они ће вам рећи тачно шта треба да радите да бисте **помогли**. На другој страни, реакција супротна овој може бити подједнако опасна. Нека деца ће покушати да беже и да се сакрију од опасне ситуације. Иако можете да будете уплашени, покушајте да останете смирени, нађите телефон и позовите **помоћ**. Као што сам раније рекао, деца често играју велику улогу у покушају **спашавања** током **хитног случаја**. Ево неколико практичних савета како данаучите децу о хитним случајевима. 1) Дубоко удахните, опустите се и покушајте да нађете **помоћ**. 2) Позовите **помоћ;** или дозивањем или телефоном. Ако неко има **рану** или је повређен, **спасилачке** екипе могу брзо да стигну. У ситуацији **опасној по живот, оператер** може да вам да постепено упутство шта да радите. 3) Никада не прекидајте везу оператеру; требају им сви детаљи о вашој тренутној локацији и **ситуацији** у којој се налазите. 4) Нађите сигурно место где ћете чекати помоћ. Не доводите себе у опасност док чекате професионалце, то ће само направити још већу **опасност**. Најбољи начин да се снађете у **опасној ситуацији** је да будете спремни за нешто тако. Ако знате шта да радите у различитим **ситуацијама**, бићете спремнији да се суочите са њима. Питајте родитеље шта да радите у случају **пожара** у кући или ако је неко из куће **повређен**. Питајте некога да вам покаже како да позовете помоћ; постарајте се да бројеви телефона **ватрогасне службе, полиције, хитне помоћи** буду меморисани у вашем телефону. Како будете старији, можете и да кренете на часове **прве помоћи**. Запамтите, у било којој **опасности**, останите смирени и позовите помоћ и не доводите себе у опасност.